AF560473

ADI SHANKARA

ADVAITA

AND YOU

ADI SHANKARA

ADVAITA

AND YOU

Suparna-Saraswati Puri

Title: Adi Shankara, Advaita and You

Author: Suparna-Saraswati Puri

ISBN: 978-93-49042-05-6

Published by:
JGS Enterprises Pvt Ltd
Imprint: The Browser

Publisher's Address:
SCO 14-15, FF, Sector 8-C, Chandigarh 160 009
Website: www.thebrowser.org
Email: service@thebrowser.org

Printed in India
© Layout and Cover Design by 99 beagles
99beagles.com

To the Moments and Masters who led
me to question
And
To Ammi-Bapu, who ensured that I
seek with complete independence

'If I have done well, and as is fitting the story, it is that which I desired: but if slenderly and meanly, it is that which I could attain unto.'

—A Hebrew Writer

Contents

Prologue

No action or thing is truly original; only the change makes it appear so. This is the case with the book in hand as well. For an intensely expansive theme of non-duality as taught by its iconic promulgator, Adi Shankara, my attempt is to connect Shankara, Advaita, and you—the reader—modern-day Vedantin, or anyone seeking clarity about oneself. Those who perceive Spirituality aerially, our mind is like a windmill that is never still. Just as with the slightest movement of the wind, the mill's wings get stirred, so does our mind, continuously flooded with thoughts. Our 'appetite for life' is responsible for the mind being incessantly at work!

Life in all its manifestations is 'inherently ritualistic' and has a presence that is from inwards to outwards. Whether it is a plant that germinates from a seed or the human form that grows out of a womb, the movement of life is the same: from inside to outside. Another and more obvious analogy is that air is imperative for the stage-wise advancement of a life-form; for human beings, spiritual pursuit is an intrinsic urge. Interestingly, this has gained momentum even more in the 'media-based world' that we live in, where there is 'an image for every moment, a feeling for every experience'.

The well-known economist, Gurcharan Das, in *The Difficulty of Being Good*, observes, 'What makes for uncertainty in our lives is often our own frailties.' The statement appears accurate in the context of materialistic accumulation and its outcome. An increased inclination towards wanting more than one's requirement, and the reliance on the notion that acquisition provides a sense of comfort, are a few of the misgivings of the existing times. Curiously, this is so when more often than usual, an inquirer prefers to describe himself or herself as 'a unique, autonomous, morally responsible human being whose inner life can be known through introspection' (Gurcharan Das).

Interestingly, when studied and reflected through the arterial network of our ancient scriptures, it leads to the idea of wellness or the state of well-being, which is self-evident. The transliteration of the English word 'wellness' to its Sanskrit equivalent is *Kaushalyam*, *Susthiti*, *Sugati*, and *Swaasth*. The last of these four means health, which, as per the ancient texts, refers to 'getting rooted in Self' (*Swa* = Self). India's natural assets are recognised as some of the most ancient formations of mountains and river valleys, which are still worshipped today as places of spiritual potency.

The famous American author Tom Wolfe wrote in one of his popular works titled *Mauve Gloves & Madmen, Clutter & Vine*, that 'the old alchemical dream was changing base metals into gold. The new alchemical dream is: changing one's personality—remaking, remodelling, elevating, and polishing one's very self'. In other words, a constant sense of burden that is experienced with the endless schedule of to-dos necessitated by the World of Liabilities we live in. However, 'Mystics and sages maintain that human consciousness necessarily evolves in the direction of transcendence of duality. This, they say, is what spiritual "seeking"—the seeking of God or "truth"—is all about' (Ali Ansari).

Evidently, the past indicates sufficiently that it has been 'man's obligation to explore the most difficult questions in the clearest possible way and use reason and intellect to arrive at the best answer' (Stewart Gordon). The ancient times witnessed a great many experiments; some were born of the years, others matured in that time; in either case, the outcome had profound revelations that aimed at change for centuries to come. The Indian sages, seers, and scriptures mastered the domain of Self-realisation, as is evident from the knowledge of the *Vedas* that contributed to the walk within.

From then to now, experiments in realising the knowledge about the Self continue to engage both the sceptics and the spiritually aware. 'This erring race of human beings dreams always of perfecting their environment by the machinery of government and society; but it is only by the perfection of the soul within that the outer environment can be perfected' (Sri Aurobindo and The Mother).

Without a doubt, it is daunting to attempt an engagement with the phenomenon of the Unseen; that which redefines dimensions and inexplicably stretches a human being's entirety beyond comprehensible levels of profundity. In my experience, often while engaging with Spirituality, terminology seems rather inadequate, and one is apparently driven towards using that of which one knows less or nothing; 'What we know is a drop, what we don't know is an ocean' (Isaac Newton). Hesitation to tread, confusion about approach, and general apprehension are some of the spontaneous indicators that come in the way of learning to let go.

Painstakingly, a stern lesson is thus imparted: 'Simply having knowledge doesn't arm one against the caprices of the soul' (Anuja Chandramouli). It would help to understand the book in hand better if you approach the subject in terms of 'Full Health', meaning the well-being of mind, body, and soul. According to the Vedantic Solution, 'Life is already involved in Matter and Mind in Life because in essence Matter is a form of veiled Life; Life is a form of veiled consciousness.'

It may be of interest to know that the premise of the book in hand is not to delve into an anthropological inquiry about faith or belief; in fact, contrarily, the attempt is to examine the exponential relevance of a highly specialised and powerful instrument of knowing, Advaita—one that delivers Self-realisation while providing clarity on existential queries regarding birth, life, pain, death, and thereafter. The book is an attempt to understand the need to think for yourself, develop practical techniques for a well-being living, and realise what matters truly. From birth till death, 'Our responsibility is simply to give our best.... Everything we do should be judged by how much it adds to the unity of life. If it conduces to unity, the work is spiritual' (Eknath Easwaran).

In an attempt to invite a wide-based, unbiased, and open-minded readership, I've experimented with scripting experiential episodes (titled 'Practical Vedanta') at the end of each chapter, in the hope that the book proves to be worthy of some reflection and introspection, rather than merely a textual engagement. The borrowing of Swami Vivekananda's powerful expression, 'Practical Vedanta', voices my own comprehension of 'self-belief', of 'self-acceptance', and the 'errors' realised.

It would be useful to mention at this point, also, what this work attempts to address. Firstly, the treatment and perspective taken towards the subject is a departure from the kinds that exist regarding the spectrum of the theme studied and interpreted.

Secondly, the endeavour is not to exhibit scholarship on the subject but to make it relatable and practical. The clichéd phrase—'to be sorted'—requires an authentic evaluation by those of us who seek solutions to a messy living. The impending relevance of Adi Shankara and his thought has come to be of profound importance to me, and it is my understanding that communicating this learning in the present environment holds immense significance as well as promise.

Lastly, as the author of the book, I admit to being no authority on Spirituality and Philosophy. Driven by a self-coined dictum, *You Are What You Seek*, the exercise is to merely share an overview of an Idea (of non-duality—Advaita) that begets an existential investigation. It helps to know what (or who) you are before undertaking a walk in any direction, for anything. Personally, the exploration through the writing of this work facilitated more than expected and enhanced a deeper outlook towards seeking.

Now remains *the* question: Why Adi Shankara's Advaita? This was the commissioned theme assigned to me eight years ago. However, the unforeseen circumstances and predicaments that the pandemic unleashed provided a more insightful explanation to me, as a first-time author. Personally, the step taken in this direction resulted in a game-changer in every possible way. It revealed truths that enabled the student of history (in me) to take on a philosophically challenging subject (Adi Shankara's Advaita) with a reasonable degree of confidence and clarity.

Also, beyond any doubt, I wholeheartedly submit that 'the doctrine advocated by Sankara is, from a purely philosophical point of view, and apart from all theological considerations, the most important and interesting one which has arisen on Indian soil; neither those forms of the Vedanta which diverge from the view represented by Sankara, nor any of the non-Vedantic systems can be compared with the so called orthodox Vedanta in boldness, depth, and subtlety of speculations' (George Thibaut).

'samsarahetunivrttisadhanabrahmatmaikatvabidyapratipattaye'

The only realisation an individual must seek is that the identity of his soul is with Brahman, the only means of his liberation from samsara.

—Adi Shankaracharya,
Brahma Sutra Bhasya (1.i.1.).

CHAPTER 1

Cause and Effect

'All that we need learn is the Book of Man, for the greatest study of man is man.'

—Kirpal Singh

It is instinctive for human beings to confront that which goes beyond them and investigate deeper realms. Influences and impressions are significant in the life of an individual (*Jiva)*. In my opinion, an identity (*astitva*) is shaped by the cognitive as well as the abstract, intrinsically. The Nobel Laureate Elie Wiesel aptly encapsulates: 'Most people think that shadows follow, precede, or surround beings or objects. The truth is that they also surround words, ideas, desires, deeds, impulses, and memories.' Apparently, the highest level of logic appears to reign in society today, and yet, there is an equally great absence of meaning. The need to practice balance in thought, mind, and action is recklessly replaced by an urge to exploit. Metaphorically speaking, Man knows that he is, but not that he has to be.

Philosophical inquiry is the 'freight and baggage underlying the politics of the day', and History substantiates it. Early India experienced a transformation in the model of knowledge prevalent. 'The nature of the change was a shift from the acceptance of the *Vedas* as revealed and as controlled by ritual to the possibility that knowledge could derive from intuition, observation, and analysis' (Romila Thapar). The new doctrine of the *Upanishads* saw the individual as the 'seeker of immortality through his own efforts' (Thapar). More importantly, the apprehension was not for heaven (*baikunth*) but for liberation or salvation—*moksha*. Spiritual evolution sought liberation of the soul—an idea related to the concept of *Atman-Brahman*. Adi Shankara writes in one of his *bhasya-s*, 'Our experience of the world is one continuous experience of *Brahman*.'

na sato vidyate bhavo
na bhavo vidyate satah
ubhayor api drsto'ntas tv
anayos tattvadarsibhih

Of the non-existent, there is no coming to be;
of the existent, there is no ceasing to be.
The conclusion about these two has been
perceived by the seers of truth.

—*Bhagavadgita, II, 16*

The historical background to the *Upanishads* depicts a society that was no longer predominantly that of cattle herding, as cultivation and commerce became heightened spheres of activity. The individual emerged as the subject seeking knowledge and liberation (Thapar).

There is a proverbial saying in Vedanta, 'What is lost by ignorance was never lost, what is gained by knowledge, always exists.' Or as Jane Cleary (Jannanji) says, 'The gain of the infinite is an infinite gain and loss of the infinite is an infinite loss.' For any kind of difficult task, a comprehensive preparation of an individual's whole being is necessary. This initiates an understanding of the casually used term, mind. For an attempt that engages in the study of the mind, clarity of terms is crucial. The mind, for instance, as an organ, 'when it has the mode of self-consciousness', is called *ahamkar* (self-sense), and it is separate from *garva* (self-consciousness).

When the mind 'has the mode of determination', it is '*buddhi*, or understanding, and attention (*citta*), when it has the mode of concentration and remembrance. The function of *citta* is important from the point of view of worship, where contemplation and concentration are essential' (Radhakrishnan). The individual's mind, its modes of *ahamkar*, *buddhi*, *citta*, and modifications or *vrtti* are collectively responsible for thoughts, ideas, and feelings in the physical body (*deha sarira*). Unless controlled through instruction, these are chiefly responsible for his suffering (*dukkha*).

Adi Shankara's Advaita places ignorance at the core of the existential discourse and *ahamkar* as its 'insubstantial' resultant. Sri Ramakrishna termed 'all individual "I"s (egos), as "unripe I"'. In essence, ego signifies whatever you think about your own little self. It is the conception of all that an individual unknowingly attributes to himself or herself as a person; it may be good or bad or fragile or fluid, etc. Incidentally, Jean-Paul Sartre, in his tiny treatise titled *The Transcendence of the Ego*, writes, 'I am my consciousness of me.' The statement refers to the notion of the higher self and the lower self, wherein 'I' refers to pure consciousness and 'me' to the ego sense. Interestingly, similarities can be observed between Shankara's Advaita and Sartre's phenomenological studies.

The following two verses from Shankara's oft-quoted work titled *Vivekacunamani,* accentuate the nature of 'self-sense' and its impact on the mind-body framework called *upadhi*:

(i)
yova pure so'hamiti pratito
buddhya praklrptastamasa' timudhaya I
tasyaiva nihsesataya vinase
brahmatmabhavah pratibandhasunyah II

That which has been created by the buddhi,
extremely deluded by nescience
and which is perceived in this body as 'I am such and such'—
when that egoism is totally destroyed,
one attains an unobstructed identity with the Brahman.

(ii)
kamah krodha lobhadambhadyasuya
hankarersyamatsaradyastu ghorah I
dharma ete rajasah pumpravrttir
yasmadesa tadrajo bandhahetuh II

> Lust, anger, avarice, arrogance, spite, egoism,
> envy, and jealousy etc.—
> These are the dire attributes of rajas,
> from which this worldly tendency of man is produced.
> Therefore, rajas is a cause of bondage.

Scriptures, sages, and seers have provided various explanations regarding themes that alternate between the search for reality and the alchemies of life. Methods for seeking are countless, but what matters is to ascertain the worth of the 21,600 breath-rhythms that nature has accorded to Man. For that 'a creative thinker of the first rank', Adi Shankara and *his* Advaita pave the way.

For an aspirant equipped with spiritual fortitude, the first step towards Vedanta is of inquiry; related to primal doubts of *Who Am I, What is the purpose of life, How the world came into existence*, and so on. Adi Shankara's Advaita 'systematically' provides answers to such queries, distils the irrelevant from the essential, and leads the way for enlightenment while living. His brilliance lies in the fact that he 'entered the philosophic inheritance of his age, and reinterpreted it with special reference to its needs' (Radhakrishnan).

Given that the book in hand is not intended to be a subject of a religious nature, the material presented is an effort to use reason and scripture for understanding both Adi Shankara and his school of Advaita. Further, it does not contradict science, logic, and empirical knowledge. One would imagine that to a thinking mind, these are the prerequisites necessary for an investigation of the Self, which Shankara addresses, on occasions, as '*Buddhi Sakshi*' (Witness of Intellect).

Spiritual philosophy can be an exacting exercise, as can the study of Advaita Vedanta to an aspirant. A reputed scholar of Indian Philosophy, G.R. Malkani, while deliberating on non-dual Vedanta, mentions that 'it is a statement of fact. There is nothing to disagree in Advaita. It cannot be refuted. It is a way of seeing.' More importantly, this specific branch of thinking does not aim to convince the inquirer about *Brahman*. It indicates the 'intuitive grasp' made possible through experience after due contemplation of Scripture (the *Upanishads*).

It is necessary to keep sight of the fact that Advaita is not a belief system that posits faith as a prerequisite for seeking salvation promised after death. Lifting the veil of ignorance to know your authentic Self, 'right here, right now', is a fundamental tenet of non-duality wherein true existence and intelligence are coalesced. Interestingly, one of the most popular philosophical discussions in recent times across international academia is about the 'Hard Problem of Consciousness'. 'There is nothing that we know more intimately than conscious experience, but there is nothing that is harder to explain' (David J. Chalmers). Evidently, Albert Einstein was able to prove that energy cannot be created nor can it be destroyed; it only changes in appearance. In a way, this only substantiates that engagement with the deeply mystical concern regarding the Self remains a constant endeavour, through the passage of time, irrespective of the advancements and developments of scientific probe in the present century.

For any kind of communication to commence, clarity of language is necessary, as 'there are many levels of language; each level giving its own insight into the "situation"' (Murty). For instance, Chalmers opines that 'Consciousness' is an ambiguous term, referring to many different phenomena that can be broadly titled as 'easy' and 'hard' phenomena of Consciousness. In the case of the former, explanation is possible using a scientific approach, hence, 'there is no real issue'. He further states that the really hard problem of consciousness is the problem of experience. When we think and perceive, there is a world of information-processing, but there is also a subjective aspect. This subjective aspect is experience.

The fundamentals of Advaita Vedanta are:

i. *Brahman* is the Ultimate Reality (Absolute Truth) and is of the nature of consciousness and bliss.

ii. Due to its *Maya* the Real appears as the world of plurality.

iii. There is absolutely no difference between *Brahman* and the individual (*Jiva*). The scriptures proclaim, 'Reality, knowledge, and infinity are *Brahman*', and Adi Shankara, in the *bhasya* (commentary) on the first *Brahma Sutra*, affirms that one who desires to know *Brahman* must undertake an inquiry concerning *Brahman*, following the study of the Upanishadic texts.

Etymologically, *Brahman* is derived from a root which signifies 'greatness' and unsurpassed greatness, because no other words or topic limit that sense' (Murty). In order to understand what Swami Sarpavpriyananda aptly calls 'the Language of Paradox in Advaita', the inquirer may find it necessary to address the following questions:

i. Why is there a need for paradox as a way to communicate?

ii. Why is it that while discussing the *Atman-Brahman* phenomenon, description through words is inadequate?

iii. How does such a communication provide spiritual insight?

In his *bhasya* on *Mandukya* Upanishad, Adi Shankara declares that *Brahman* is supposed to be beyond language. With his deftness in logic, he elucidates that the need for language arises with the presence of any of the five factors, namely, class (*jati*); attribute (*guna*); function/action (*krirya*); relation (*sambandh*); and convention (*rudri*). Since these parameters of description do not apply to Pure Consciousness, the use of language as we know it cannot be applied for describing and explaining the nature of *Brahman*.

The Great Master, Adi Shankara, goes on to clarify the inexplicable ways used by the rishis in the *Vedas* and *Upanishads*. For instance, in the Brihadaryanka Upanishad, *Brahman* has been defined by the apophatic method (*neti neti*—not this not this). Another way is through implied meaning, as in the case of the prophetic Upanishadic statements known as *Mahavakya*—I am *Brahman*. In his *Dakshinamurti Stotra,* Shankara explains the methodology of silence (*maunam vyakhyanam*) used by a teacher to describe Pure Consciousness to his disciples.

maunavyakhyaprakatatiaparabrahmatattvam yuvanam
varsisthantevasadrsiganairavravrtam brahmanisthaih I
acaryendram karakalitatacinmudramanandamurtim
sva maramam muditavadanam daksinamurtimide II

I praise Shri Dakshinamurti, my youthful teacher, who, through silent instruction, reveals the truth of Parabrahman: who is surrounded by aged disciples, mighty sages devoted to Brahman. I praise the supreme teacher, the essence of bliss, who revels in his own self, the silent one, whose hand is uplifted in the benediction of knowledge.

It would be relevant to state at this point that, according to Adi Shankara's Advaita, the term ignorance (*adhyasa; avidya*) is crucial because it is, as the Oxford Dictionary of Hinduism states, 'the persistent tendency, through superimposition (*adhyasa*), to mistake appearance for reality'. He explains *adhyasa* as taking something to be what it is not. In *Vedanta Sutra*, (Vol. I. p. 6), Shankara explains *avidya* (non-knowledge or ignorance) as, 'This superimposition, thus defined, learned men consider to be *Avidya*, and the ascertainment of the true nature of that which is (the Self) by means of the discrimination of that (which is superimposed on the Self) they call Knowledge (*Vidya*).' In other words, as long as the individual imagines himself to be different from his real Self—*Brahman*, he is in a state of ignorance. When he can say Aham Brahmasmi, 'I am *Brahman*', then he possesses knowledge in the truest sense and is the enlightened being, free absolutely.

More importantly, 'in Vedanta there is no notion of "sin" other than *avidya*, or ignorance' (Veena Sharma). Adi Shankara was convinced that the removal of *avidya* was best addressed with 'the language of paradox', an effective means of communication. Experience (*anubhava*), imagination (*kalpana*), or memory (*smarana*) is the theory of knowledge that pivots on the harmony of *the* spiritual understanding, i.e., the knower and the known.

As suggested earlier, words and terms applied in Advaita bear subtle and specific meanings. For instance, 'the word "*jnanam*", or knowledge, does not refer to a process of knowing, a knowledge *of* something, or even the act of thinking, all of which arise and disappear. It refers to an inherent awareness or consciousness which is the very ground in which thinking occurs' (Veena Sharma).

In that sense, knowledge branches into *vrtti* and *swaroop*. That which reveals the object (*visaya*) is known as *vrtti*, which also means modifications of the sense organ we call mind; while *swaroopa* is Consciousness in its own nature. Vedanta is *vrtti jnana* about *swaroop jnana*. In aggregate, knowledge is the sum total of *vrtti*, that is, pervasion of mind as an object and *phalla vyapti*, that is, pervasion of Pure Consciousness. Therefore, the ultimate reality—'*Brahman* is not a subject matter of faith, but of "discovery" through knowledge.'

Jiva, the individual (as an entity), 'is a construct embedded in the metaphysical conception of the universe visualised by this system of knowledge'. Under the 'Vedanta lens', he is composed of the following dimensions: (i) gross/physical body (*sthool sarira*); (ii) subtle body/ mind (*sukshmasarira*), and (iii) causal body (*karana sarira*). The basis of name and form (*nama-roopam*), commonly addressed as the 'Identity' of an individual in the world/universe (*Jagat*), stems from the gross and subtle body. However, it is 'mistaken identity', because the real identity of the being is, in fact, the third, *karana sharira*, which is YOU—the non-dual Self ('*poornatvam*'). 'As Reality itself, the human is spiritual and partakes of the freedom which characterises Ultimate Reality' (Veena Sharma).

> *karye hi karanam pasyetpascatkaryam visarjayet,*
> *karanatvam tato nasyedavasistam bhavenmunih. (139)*
>
> One should see cause in the effects and
> then should discard the effects altogether.
> Then the cause also should be dissolved,
> then what remains is the Truth Absolute,
> And the seek becomes verily that.
>
> —*Adi Shankaracharya,*
> *Aparokshanubhuti*

We know, but more often than usual choose not to realise, thereby accepting to be ignorant willingly; thus inviting sorrow and pain, thereby perpetuating suffering. Spiritualising everyday living is practising Vedanta, says Swami Sarvapriyananda, a learning that has desirously made me want to grow inward. Indeed, it takes mature souls and *yuga purushas* like Gautam Buddha, Adi Shankara, and Swami Vivekananda to remind us that 'Freedom is the first condition of growth'.

Practical Vedanta: *My Tenets*

Readers who have managed to reach this far, to you, my heartfelt thank you! To me, an acute comprehension of 'Cause and Effect' manifested during the dystopic period of the twelve months between 2020 and 2021. A constant sense of inadequacy, erratic behaviour, and a hapless sense took charge of my name and form self. It left me questioning and seeking tangible solutions. However, a niggling subtle assertion that I have not been abandoned or un-looked-after, made its presence felt especially through the lockdowns. As a result of the physical, emotional, and intellectual gruelling that I experienced, certain thoughts cropped up one morning. Without hesitation or preparation, I penned the same, as they rolled out on my mental scape.

My Tenets, as I like to call the statements, settled me then and have since continued to provide strength and sight, whenever I am suffering:

- I am Nobody but You.
- There is no Me in I.
- Enjoy silence more.
- Laugh more and complain less.
- Nothing is forever.
- Life is Theatre, so cut the drama.
- Forget all that is Unnecessary.
- You can live without anger, but not without Love.
- Wear your talents lightly.
- Respect limitations and Move Ahead.

The Vedantic learning in the above-mentioned tenets conveyed quite emphatically to me: 'Through self-effort alone you will unfold your real Self'; and to that extent, the above-mentioned truths illuminate the route I take as a doer.

CHAPTER 2

You Are What You Seek

'True happiness, we are told, consists in getting out of one's self; but the point is not only to get out—you must stay out; and to stay out you must have some absorbing errand.'

—Henry James, Roderick Hudson (1875)

In the Indian tradition, one of the better-known reasons for the interest and inclination towards Spirituality is that it provides an integrated framework with options to choose from. For believers of faith, the search for 'the notion of a reality abiding amidst all change' is possible through *Bhakti* (devotion). To the mystically inclined, the path of *Yoga* (meditation) appeals as a methodology for Self-realisation. For those who select *vicara* (inquiry) as the *modus operandi,* Advaita is the foundation for Self-realisation. A significant trigger that directs attention inwards is a natural pursuit for 'something that is lasting', while living every moment enveloped in impermanence. Yet, 'we are so conditioned to believe that happiness can be gained by accumulating money and manipulating others that we can't see how ridiculous a belief this is' (Easwaran).

A barrage of questions plagues the mind. From asking, what *is* life all about, to is there a way to remain happy constantly, to what does peace of mind really feel like, to how to cope with the eventuality of death, and many more. Answers lie in Vedanta. It explains and offers practices that enable us to navigate the dynamic force called Life. Vedantic reasoning makes the chaos in our homes, offices, and elsewhere not only manageable but ineffective. 'Whatever knowledge Vedanta places before you, examine it *per se.* Analyse it yourself. Apply your power of discrimination to it. Assimilate it. Put it into practice. Verify it in your own life. Thus, make it your own. Truth is your own' (Parthasarathy).

It is a fact that constant preoccupation with the body-mind complex leads to incessant suffering and unavoidable pain. Vedanta terms this complex as *upadhi*, as it 'comes and goes' and as a result unleashes a continuum of miseries that are categorised: those miseries born of an unknown source or cosmic (*adhidaivika*), those of a known (object) source or worldly pleasures (*adhibhautika*), and those of the (subject) individual's body-mind complex (*adhyatmika*).

The erroneous perception of the object (*uppadhi*) is a depreciating asset that undergoes a six-fold change from seed to dust, while the subject (*Atman-Brahman*) remains unchanging and eternal. The consequence of *avidya* (erroneous perception) gives rise to the 'mistake' that the human being is not free. The very purpose of seeking (*Brahman jnana*) is to 'correct the error' and be liberated. Adi Shankara realised the urge to spread the awakening knowledge, particularly at a time when the people of a uniquely divergent land were confused and lost, above all, spiritually.

'The Advaitism of Samkara is a system of great speculative daring and logical subtlety. Its austere intellectualism, its remorseless logic, which marches on indifferent to the hopes and beliefs of man, its relative freedom from theological obsessions, make it a great example of a purely philosophical scheme' (Radhakrishnan). Until the engagement with Vedanta remains uninitiated, for most of us, it is distant and difficult to understand that knowledge and experience are separate. We think we know, but we don't—more often than usual. A crucial inquiry in Advaita is the difference between knowledge—*jnanam*—and experience—*anubhava.* 'You must try to combine in your life immense idealism with immense practicality... the method of man-making. The true *man* is he who is strong as strength itself and yet possesses a woman's heart.' (Swami Vivekananda, *Sannyasa: Its Ideal and Practice*). In other words, actions must not be only self-serving in intent and purpose; correctness must be at the core. It may sound idealistic, however, it bears practical implementation. What is needed for such an accomplishment is controlling the mind, which 'hardly remains in the present'. That is where the Vedanta (inclusive of Advaita) plays a pivotal role. 'It is with your personal experience you delve deeper into the truths of Vedanta. You attain peace and happiness' (Parthasarthy).

According to Vedanta, the Truth—*Sat* is categorised into *Vyavaharika, Paramarthika*, and *Pratibhasika*, also understood as the three modes of existence. Mistaking the rope to be a snake is *pratibhasika sat;* responding to the world/universe as real is *vyavaharika sat*, and that *Brahman* is the only Reality, is *paramarthika sat.* In order to realise his real self, the inquirer of Advaita is pointed towards the three-fold contemplation: to 'listen' (*sravana*), to 'practice' (*manana*), and to 'meditate' (*nididhysana*) upon scriptural wisdom (*sruti jnana*).

Known to encourage inquiry through the mode of question-answer, Advaitin Shankara points in the text *Prasnottara-Ratna-Malika*:

kim samsare saram?
bahuso'api vicintyamanam idam-eva I
kim manujesvista-tamam?
sva-para-hitay'odyatam janma II

What is the essential lesson to be understood
about this trans migratory life?
The understanding that it is transitory
(lasting only for a few moments).
What should be the dearest thing for man?
The attainment of a life that is entirely
devoted to the good of oneself and others.

A life based on conflict cannot experience and spread harmony; addressing the 'basis for environmental awareness and ethics', Advaita lays foundational emphasis on values such as simple living, frugality, compassion, and non-violence. The validity of specified do's (*vidhi*) and don'ts (*nishedh*) while performing actions (*karma*) as recorded in the scriptures, is a tried and tested tradition practised by aspirants, inquirers, and Vedantins.

In his *Upadeshasahsari,* Adi Shankara explains with the following verse:

vidyayah pratikulam hi karma syatsabhimanatah I
nirvikaratmabuddhisca vidyetiha prakirtita II

> Accompanied by egoism, actions are incompatible with knowledge. For it is well known here (in the Vedantas) that knowledge is the consciousness, that the self is changeless.

It is important to grasp that non-duality never denies the individual's experience of the world (defined by plurality). On the contrary, the lived experience and its analysis, as illustrated in the Taittiriya and Aitereya Upanishads and, more concisely, in the *Mandukya* Upanishad, question the reality of that plurality.

In an environment stimulated by instant deliverability, Adi Shankara's *jnana* is a customised version for the inquirer who seeks to relinquish a fraudulent notion of living. The Great Master's life and teachings exemplify the analytical evaluation of the existential probe '*Koh*N' (Who Am I). Shankara's structural construct, based entirely on reason and the revelation of scriptures, is abundant with simple yet subtle practices that can be performed by a householder as well as a hermit. He developed his *vicara* because, 'philosophically, he became convinced that no movement could thrive on a spirit of negation, and so asserted the reality of *Brahman* on the basis of Sruti'. Having lived in a period that witnessed significant 'shifts' in tradition, Adi Shankara's methodology of arguments is termed as '*prasannam gambhirya*', meaning elegant yet rich and simple; the construct stands apart on an ontological landscape that resonates of clear and direct instruction.

Acharya Shankara, in his *Upadesha Panchkama Stotra*, also known as *Sadhana Panchakam*, writes:

> *vedo-nityam-adheeyatam*
> *taduditam karmasvanushteeyatam*
>
> Let the scriptures be studied daily
> Let those Karmas enjoined in the
> scriptures be well performed

Practical Vedanta: *'Jaano ya Manno'*

Getting acquainted with Adi Shankara and his Advaita has had me embroiled in long-drawn spells of doubt and procrastination. Being a student of history, at the time the task was offered of writing a book on Shankara and his Advaita, the clichéd question—why me—did raise its head. With an ocean of literature that exists on the great thinker and his philosophy, what was I going to contribute to the subject? How would I manage the much-needed research, given my ignorance of Sanskrit? Such apprehensions clouded my mind and consumed me with intimidation and fear.

I was dually tested, thrown in various directions, and had to acknowledge that my engagement with the manuscript was intended far beyond the self-gratification of authoring a piece of writing. In order to proceed with the task assigned, I needed to grasp with utmost earnestness that the rigmarole involved was for my well-being and spiritual growth. It is an outlook that I've come to realise since and apply whenever needed with complete acceptance and surrender. The clarity that I sought lay in facing the fears that had withheld me. The idea of failing blinded the path (of wellness) that had been marked for my onward journey. I recalled the proverbial saying in Hindi, *'Mushkil museebat tab banti hai, jab hum mushkil ko hal karne ki kriya chode dein'.* The primary research needed for the book was for me to examine (Jaano) myself, wholeheartedly, with warts and all. It warranted an objective gaze across episodes that had taken place and were actually milestones for change in my life. It was not an easy endeavour. But then, can any kind of investigation regarding oneself be simple and unproblematic?

I avoided overthinking while making a habit of addressing the moment (Now). Observing activities in the natural environs of my dwelling became a classroom for reflection. Gurus came in different forms, and I (as a novice) began with the most difficult job ever—to see inward; look within.

The lessons made it evident that preparation to write on non-duality commands—to let go of the controls; to exist in complete surrender of the small I—Self; to ungrudgingly accept all that comes your way. Most importantly, allow more of your intuition to determine your decisions and let your mind rest. Also, the willingness to learn from every experience proved to be a healthy addition. It is a fact that 'the first principle of true teaching is that nothing can be taught'. I realised.

CHAPTER 3

Adi Shankara's Advaita

'Failing to realise your Self is indeed an inconceivable loss.'
—Kena Up.II: 5

The story of Adi Shankara (788 AD–820 AD) can be viewed as a manual that details eloquently the philosophy of communication with the Self. It began with his birth in Kaladi (Kerala), followed by renunciation in his youth, 'on fire with intellectual ambition', sharpened under the tutelage of Guru Govindapada at Omkareshwar, Madhya Pradesh. Thereafter, *sanyasin* Shankara travelled extensively the length and breadth of the sub-continent, 'to impress on the people a sense of unity'. Popular as 'a stiff and intrepid debater', he successfully carried the mission 'to expose the contradictions of life and thought with an unmatched incisiveness'. For his adversaries, Shankara's 'shrewd political genius' combined with his tender age was a challenge they had no choice but to meet. On completing his task, legend has it that the Great Master mysteriously disappeared into the elusiveness of the Himalayas, at Kedarnath (Kashmir).

There is evidence to substantiate the deserved glory bestowed upon the exceptional renouncer. 'It has been declared that at the age of sixteen, he (Sankara) had completed all his writings' (Swami Vivekananda). However, it is Adi Shankara's extraordinary presence across academic disciplines and domains of inquiry as a scholar, 'a philosopher, a poet, a savant, and a saint, a mystic and religious reformer' that sets him apart and in a league of his own. An oft-quoted hymn of salutation for Adi Shankara reads as:

> *srutismritipurananam alayam karunalayam,*
> *namami bhagavadpadam sankaram lokasankaram.*
>
> I prostrate to Adi Shankaracharya,
> an incarnation of Lord Shiva,
> who is responsible for the welfare of the universe,
> is the repository of the Divine Knowledge of *Vedas*,
> *Upanishads* and who is the embodiment of mercy.

Interestingly, through the annals of History and Indian Thought, Adi Shankara enjoys an exalted status and continues to be a personage of interest. Primarily because 'every system of thought is determined not only by the positive content which it attempts to express, but also by the views which it wishes to oppose'. For Shankara, the study of the fundamental nature of knowledge, reality, and existence 'is not an intellectual pursuit but a dedicated life'. The entire spectrum of his copious literature is absorbed in intense and refined thinking. Yet, each specimen is written in Sanskrit that bears a poetic expression, lucidity, and a cogently integrated matrix of concepts, occasionally of non-Advaitic schools of thought.

The ontological purity of Adi Shankara's Advaita appeals to the seeker who walks away from the trappings of a belief system. His is a method (drawn upon the *Upanishads*) that is accurate, aimed with focused investigation of the human behaviour, in the tangible sphere of 'here and now'. In this way, the Great Master proves to be a *marg darshak,* viewed by some as a towering spiritual facilitator instrumental in rediscovering the true nature of one's being. The rationale of his non-dual philosophy pierces through dogmatic prejudices that may produce fear of any kind, in the heart and mind of an aspirant, devotee, or seeker alike. 'Reactions are a source of suffering,' and Advaita Vedanta enables the *Jiva* to be serene and strong at the same time.

Radhakrishnan observes that the Jagat Guru (Adi Shankara), 'with his acute feeling of the immeasurable world, stirring gaze into the abysmal mysteries of spirit, his unswerving resolve to say neither more nor less than what could be proved, stands out as a heroic figure of the first rank in the somewhat motley crowd of the religious thinkers of medieval India'. To the global community of students, the Great Master's appeal is persistent as a fuss-free *Acharya* (teacher) whose doctrine of non-duality engages their curious intellect because of its penetrating logic, precise argument based on scripture, radical thought, and an unmistakable sense of humour. Shankara was aware that 'when attempting to persuade someone about a topic on which they already have a firm stance, it is important to know the facts about the topic and know your audience and what is important to them'.

In recent times, another expanding category of enthused inquirers is an amalgam of entrepreneurs, corporate professionals, and working women, for whom paucity of time reigns supreme. To them, Shankara comes across as a voice championing strong ideals, of uninhibited disposition with zero tolerance for falsity or pretention. Lastly, to his wide range of devotees and emerging followers, the Great Master is the *Rishi-Yogi* whose life's work is *the* principle that enlightens the *Jiva* about his being 'Infinite Consciousness Bliss' (*Satchitanand*).

In *Bhaja Govindam*, verse 11, Adi Shankara says:

ma kuru dhana-jana-yauvana-garvam
harati nimesat kalah sarvam I
maya-mayam idam akhilam hitva
brahma-padam tvam pravisa viditva II

Boast not of youth or friends or wealth;
Swifter than eyes can wink,
by Time each one of these is stolen away.
Abjure the illusion of the world
And join yourself to timeless Truth.

Greatness is a retrospective confer. Its intended meaning is significantly enhanced in the context of Shankara and his concept of Advaita. The visual representation of the sub-continent referred to as '*bharat-varsha*' during his lifetime differed substantially from the geographical country known as India. The famed land enjoyed a wealth of diversity in its *darshanik-vicara*, mystic allure, beliefs, and cultural traditions drawn from 'irreconcilable worldviews—from the Buddhists, the Mimansakas (old

Vedic householders), and the Vedantins (the later Vedic hermits) to the Shaivas, the Vaishnavas, and the Shaktas'. The Great Master observes in his *bhashya* on the *Brahma Sutra* (1.3.33), 'One can say that there never was a universal ruler as there is none now.'

Recognised widely for being a visionary, Shankara organised the chaos that he encountered by laying the foundation (*adharshila*) of a renewed system of spiritual practice. Almost seventy-two sects were codified under six headings: (1) Shaivas, (2) Vaishnavas, (3) Kaumara, (4) Sakta, (5) Ganapatiya, and (6) Saurya. Realising the urgency for a unified spiritual landscape meant to integrate the obvious diversity, Shankara established the four monastic seats of Advaita learning in the four corners of the country: Dwarka (West), Puri (East), Sringeri (South), and Badrikashrama (North). Understanding their need for a sanctuary, '*Sanman Sthapana*', the Great Master founded the *Dashanami Sampradaya* for the traditional wandering ascetics with a staff (*ekadandi sanyasis*), with access to the four Matthas. The structural remodelling done fourteen hundred years ago thrives as a living tradition in the temples of India to date.

Adi Shankara was firmly convinced that Advaita Vedanta alone could deliver 'the truth of the conflicting creeds'. Thus, the only purpose of his 'copious literary outpourings' was to help the *jiva* become aware of his real nature (*Brahman*) and free himself from the web of the world (*Jagat Mithya*).

nityasuddhavimuktaikamakhandanandamadvayam I
satyam jnanamantam yatparam brahmahameva tat II

I am verily that supreme Brahman,
which is eternal, stainless, and free;
which is one, indivisible, and non-dual;
and which is of the nature of bliss, truth,
knowledge, and infinity.

Historian Romila Thapar writes in *Cultural Past*, 'Arguing for a correlation between sacrifices, resources, and innovations in belief systems is just not an economic enterprise. It is an attempt to insist that ideologies are not history-free.' Adi Shankara's Advaita is no exception. Before his arrival, there had been 'a change in the paradigm of knowledge'. The multitude of 'theistic sects' engaged in the perpetuation of ritualistic practices had brought about 'a general sense of weariness' that was rescued by the 'path of renunciation' with Buddhism and Jainism becoming popular in a Hindu nation.

As a result, the 'unusual and paradoxical presence of the renouncer, not just as a marginal feature but a person of considerable authority' became integral to the philosophical outlook of the time. It was towards the end of the early Vedic period that the primary character of the knowledge of *Sruti—iti rahasyam* (this is the secret) *iti Upanishad* (this is the Upanishad) made its presence felt, even though initially it was 'deliberately kept to a limited audience'. Subsequently, focus shifted from 'Vedic ritual practice' to inquiry into 'the immortality of soul, the realisation of the self, and belief in rebirth and retribution'. Thus empowering the individual to become a seeker of *moksha* (in relation to the concept of *Atman-Brahman*), and not the 'heaven of Indra'.

This background contributes towards Adi Shankara moving from an observer to 'a political sage engaging with and responding to the historical context of his time'.

The above explanation of events that shaped the Indian Classical thought also gave Adi Shankara a certain legitimacy to make use of effective practices while articulating the epistemology of his Advaita. For instance, the idea of 'pure consciousness' from the Samkhya order, of monastic order—*Peetha/ Matthas*—from the Buddhist *Sanghas,* Yoga techniques, the hermeneutics of the Purva Mimamsa system, and so on. However, the credit for having integrated and created a corpus of literature and finely distilled instructions remains solely with Adi Shankara, *the* spiritual leader responsible for the resurgence of a way of living; some term it as Hinduism. The following verse from *Vivekachudamani* highlights the Great Master's intent behind his Advaitic thought:

avijnate pare tattve sastradhitistu nisphala I
vijnate' pi pare tattve sastradhitistu nisphala II

The study of scriptures is useless as long
as the highest truth is unknown,
and it is equally useless when the
highest truth has already been known.

The opening statement, '*athato brahma-jijnasa*', of Adi Shankara's Adhyasa *Bhasya*, the introduction to his commentary on the *Brahma Sutra*, has been hailed by the renowned scholar of Eastern and Western thinking, J.N. Mohanty, as 'the most profound statement' that he had come across in Philosophy. The unmitigated 'audacity of thought' deliberating on the nature of consciousness initiates the discourse on *avidya*, responsible for the individual's bondage (of births and deaths) and his ultimate deliverance through '*brahmanubhava*'. Acknowledged as his magnum opus, the *bhasyakar* (commentator), Shankara, proves beyond doubt the veracity of his command of the Veda-Vedanta with the 'root-cause analysis' of samsara.

The repository of non-duality with Adi Shankara as the chief exponent upholds the maxim, '*Ekam Sat Vipra Bahuda Vadanti*' of the ancient Rishis; a metaphysical fact that continues to preoccupy scientists, philosophers, and spiritual leaders globally. In the anthology titled, *The World As I See It*, Albert Einstein states, 'The fairest thing we can experience is the mysterious. It is the fundamental emotion which stands at the cradle of true art and true science.'

The expression (*Ekam Sat...*) addresses ethics developed by tradition, particularly for the well-being of humans as well as nature. It was the unconventional thinking of these spiritual custodians (*rishi-munis*) while exploring existential queries like what am I, etc. They experienced the 'Vedantic solution that Life is already involved in Matter and Mind in Life because in essence Matter is a form of veiled life, Life a form of veiled consciousness' (*Perspectives for a New Millennium*).

There are scholars who believe that just as in Dwapara Yuga, Vyas was an absolute supreme authority on Indian thought, so is Adi Shankara in the Kali Yuga (supposedly, inclusive of the present time). Their conviction stems from the fact that epochs reveal the wisdom of the ancients through the preordained. However, to a spiritual inquirer (*adhikari*), the substantial alone satisfies; 'For essentially, all Nature seeks a harmony, life, and matter in their own sphere as much as mind in the arrangement of its perceptions'. Therefore, 'scriptural testimony' coupled with rationale and experience as advocated by the Great Master impresses deeply. 'According to Sankara, the supreme exists in percipient self. It is always the unconditioned that transcends the conditioned' (Reddy).

For an investigation of Acharya Shankara's idea of non-duality, it is necessary to possess a clear and comprehensive understanding of the narrative of Indian classical thought. He is one subject that cannot be studied in isolation, howsoever perceived; a thinker, scholar, social reformer, or revivalist.

Vedantic mysticism, Philosophy, and Adi Shankara are interconnected. Acharya's perspective originates from the *sat* that 'we are all greater than we know'. The prophetic tenor sets the stage for his Advaita to be a one-of-a-kind management system based on 'intuitive grasp' that deconstructs a seeker's apparatus of conditioned living. It is in the Rigveda that the earliest mention of Advaita, the theory of oneness, is made: 'Truth is but one; sages call It in many ways (1,22,104-46)'.

While it is vital to bear in mind that even though he was not the first advocate of non-duality, Adi Shankara is the source of an integrated thinking that navigates best with knowledge—*jnana*—as its compass. In order to understand that 'deep within us our self lives a life of which it does not speak', an outline regarding the nomenclature and concepts of his monism is suggested. An examination of Acharya's non-dual principle explains that an individual's struggle—his life—is a consequence of an erroneous perception, enhanced by desire (*kama*) that manifests in action (*karma*), resulting in bondage to the cycle of birth(s) and death(s). Hence, *jnana* needs to be understood for what it is; 'Vedanta *vicara* is synonymous with *Atmavicara*'.

Salvation from such repeated suffering is available to the inquirer, and that too while living—*Jivanmuktah.* Acharya Shankara's concept of *jivanmuktah* is the axis of happiness that is inherent to a human being as well as an insect. It is that 'entity which, if one possesses one does not seek any other. *Jiva* is the embodiment of such happiness'. In his *Prasnottara-Ratna-Malika,* verse 12, Acharya questions in his inimitable style:

ko narakah? paravasata.
kim saukhyam? sarva-sanga-viratirya. I
-kim satyam? bhuta-hitam.
priyam ca kim praninam? asavah. II 12

What is hell? The state of subjection to others.
What is happiness? The state of complete
non-attachment to everything.

What is truth? That which is beneficial to living beings.
What is dear to all creatures? Life.

To an apprentice of Vedanta, Adi Shankara suggests the 'quartet of practice', *Sadhana cathustya*—four-fold thesis as a prerequisite for removing *avidya* and stepping into the realm of Advaita Vedanta. Acharya begins with (1) *Viveka* (Discrimination) as the first qualification used to distinguish between permanent (*nitya*) that is Atmanand and the impermanent (*anitya*) that is the world-universe; followed closely by the need for (2) *Vairagya* (Dispassion) that is reflected in a pure mind that is detached from all appearances/apprehensions; and can be achieved by (3) *Shad sampatti* (six tools of discipline) that control senses and the mind and lastly, (4) *Mumukshuta*, 'an intense desire for freedom,' to liberate oneself from the birth-death *chakra*.

The Great Master, in his *Tattva-bodha*, elucidates on *samadisadhanasampattih*—the six-fold treasure—with the following verse:

samah kah? mano nigrah I
damah kah? caksuradibahyendriyanigrahah I
uparamah kah? svadharmanusthanameva I
titiksha ka? sitonasukhaduhkhadisahisnutvam I
sraddha kidrsi? guruvedantavakyadisu visvasah sraddha I
samadhanam kim? cittaikagrata I

What is sham? It is the control or mastery over the mind.
What is dam? It is the control of the external
sense organs, such as the eyes, etc.
What is uparam or uparati? It is the strict observance of
one's own dharma{duty}.
What is titiksha? It is endurance of heat and cold,
pleasure and pain, etc.
What is the nature of shraddha? Faith in the words,
etc., of the guru and Vedanta {scriptures} is shraddha.
What is samadhana? It is the single pointedness
of the mind.

Adi Shankara's teaching of Advaita is a concise practice achieved in two undisclosed stages. The premise that the inquirer is distinctly separate from *Atman* constitutes the first step known as *atman-anatman vicara.* Herein, the Jagat Guru uses relatable instances from the seeker's daily life for instructing his methodology of 'direct-realisation'. With remarkable '*Tarkasastra*' (the science of logic), he amplifies the *viveka*, differences highlighted through discussions on *drig-drishya* {subject-object}; *cit-jadda* {sentient-insentient}; *panca kosah* {the five sheaths}; *avasthatrayam* {the three states of awake, dream, and deep sleep}; *saguna-nirguna* {attribute-without attribute}; *savikar-nirvikar* {changing-unchanging); *ekam-anekam* {unified-plurality}; *antar-bahi* {inner-outer}, and so on.

In some of the *prakarana granthas,* acknowledged as the authored works of Adi Shankara, he has explicated his Advaitic thought (*vicara*) crisply in a question-and-answer format. The fact that the normative way of seeking knowledge enjoyed mass appeal was of primary concern to Adi Shankara. Similarly, the application of familiar examples of rope-snake, clay-pot, water-wave, silver-nacre, and so on, to illustrate the distinction between *Jiva* and *Atman* is reflective of his attempt to deliver Advaita at the common man's doorstep.

Verse 40 from Acharya's *Aparokshanubhuti* eloquently sums up *atman-anatman vicara*:

> *evam dehadvayadanyah atma purusa isvarah,*
> *sarvatma, sarvarupasca sarvatito'hamavyayah*
>
> Thus, I, the Purusha. am something entirely
> different from these two bodies.
> I am the Self of everything, of all forms,
> beyond everything and immutable,
> Lord of the universe.

Acharya Shankara wittingly gives a dramatic twist in the second stage and reverses the *Atman-anatman vicara* completely; 'the very existence of duality confirms the presence of suffering'. Having established *Jiva* and *Atman* as two distinctly separate entities, Shankara's *vicara* concludes by quoting the *Upanishads* to reiterate Advaita—*the* One with no second.

In response to the inquirer wondering about the validity of establishing duality only to dismiss it subsequently, the Great Master's explanation is blazing, straightforward, and simple. You, the *jiva,* ignorantly sees only the body-mind system as the Self; duality is deployed to enable you to exercise *viveka,* remove *avidya*, and establish I—*Atman*, the Knower. The *Bhagavadgita* provides a fine definition of I—the Knower, in the following verse:

ksetrajnam ca'pi mam viddhi
sarvaksetresu bharata
ksetraksetrajnayor jnanam
yat taj jnanam matam mama

Know Me as the Knower of the field
in all fields, O Bharata (Arjuna).
The knowledge of the field and its knower,
do I regard as true knowledge.

—*Chapter 13:2*

In his summation, the Acharya, using the illustrations of rope-snake, clay-pot, and so on, reiterates that *jagat* as experienced by *jiva* is nothing but *Brahman*. That '*Brahman* is name, action, and experience'; creation and destruction of *jagat* is by *Isvara* (*Brahman* with attribute) are truths that Adi Shankara delivers after distilling the lofty aphorisms of *sruti*.

At this juncture, it is vital to realise that Shankara's simple but subtle vocabulary can be misleading for a beginner. The tripod of *sravana-manana-nididhyasana* is indicative of a highly nuanced teaching in the Great Master's *vicara*. It is the sense organs (*jnanindriyas*) first that connect the inquirer with *sruti jnana*; 'receiving the wisdom on which you contemplate is called *sravana*'. Subsequently, *manana* is the deeper reflection of the wisdom with the mind's inner organs of perception (*karmindriyas*). Wisdom of That Thou Art, soaked in silence, defines *nididhyasana*.

brahmaivahamasmityaparoksajnanena
nikhilakarmabandhavinirmuktah syat I

By immediate knowledge that I am Brahman alone,
one becomes free from bondage of all karmas.

—*Adi Shankaracharya,*
Tattva-bodha

A cascade of verses composed by the Acharya in his succinct *prakarana grantha*, *Aparokshanubhuti*, substantiates beyond doubt that direct realisation is attainable by *viveka*. In the concluding section of the text, he presents an ensemble of fifteen handy techniques that are suggested to the *jiva* for *jivanmukti*.

In the light of the Advaitic premise that the 'ultimate reality is the non-dual spirit', Adi Shankara raised the edifice of his idea of Advaita on knowledge that is sourced from perception, inference, and the voice of the scriptures (*Upanishads*). His instruction broke away from the covenant of intimidating orthodoxy and its complex ritualism and sacrificial tradition. Viewed in its entirety, the spectrum of his teachings does enjoy a pan-echelon because it offers something to everybody. Shankara's Vedanta is 'a philosophical solution that lifts us, through the power of thought which alone can reconcile and ennoble the different sides of life, into the ideal of joy and peace' (Radhakrishnan).

ärdhena pravakshyämi yad-uktam granthakotibhih |
brahma satyam jagan-mithyä jivo brahmaiva näparah ||

In half of a *sloka* I state what has been stated by millions of texts;
that is, Brahman alone is real and this world is an appearance,
and *jiva* is non-different from Brahman.

Practical Vedanta: Seven *Darsanas*

It is no exaggeration that scripting each chapter of the book in hand felt like surviving a Ferris wheel that wouldn't stop. At the same time, it gave me recurring moments of inexplicable satisfaction; a feeling that echoes acutely with the following Hindi film melodies, my all-time favourites:

Kayi baar yun bhi dekhaa hai,
Ye jo man kee seemaa rekhaa hai,
Man daud ne lagataa hai.
Anjaanee pyaas ke peechhe,
Anjaanee aas ke peechhe,
Man daud ne lagataa hai.
Film – Rajanigandha

Poocho na kaise maine rain bitai,
Ik pal jaise, ik jugg beeta.
Ik pal jaise, ik jugg beeta,
Jugg bite mohe neend na aayi.
Film – Meri Surat Teri Ankhen

Mann re tu kahe na dheer dhare,
woh nirmohi Moh na jaane jinka moh kare.
Iss jivan kee chadhtee dhaltee,
Dhup ko kiss ne bandha,
Rang pe kisane pehre dale,
Rup ko kisane bandha
Kahe yeh jatan kare.
Film – Chitralekha

Over the years, I have come to understand that the presence of mind and common sense are inherent gifts, at our disposal 24x7. Using them frequently and effectively solves many situations that may otherwise seem difficult to address. I experienced this, especially, during the three months of 2020 while writing the manuscript. Attending to everything by myself and being alone was not a first for me; it was the time made available to me for scripting on Adi Shankara and Advaita that proved to be extraordinary.

The surreality in the environment was palpable. While the world grappled with the gravity of an unfamiliar state, providence ensured that I utilise the span with That which determines everything. However, it wasn't all that easy! September 2020 showcased seven 'darsanas' across seven days. For me, it was an examination to assess how qualified and competent I was to engage with Adi Shankara and Advaita. From confronting the smallest of my fears (particularly of snakes and slithery reptiles) to dealing with the demise of a dear one, it seemed a 24-hour examination was underway, wherein the ability to confront, cope, and carry on was being assessed by the powers that be.

There is no vocabulary that would do justice to my experience of those seven 'darsanas', in seven days. Nevertheless, the week that was survived resulted in the following learning:

- What do we know?
- How little we know about ourselves.
- What is Reality?
- What is Knowledge – how do you know anything?
- What is the point of it all?

Eknath Easwaran encapsulates it beautifully in his book, *Vishnu and His 1000 Names*, when he says, 'The problem is our idea of the human being. We think we are very limited creatures, very small, good for maybe only fifteen minutes of love or patience before we have to crack. Instead of identifying with our deepest Self, we are identifying with some biochemical-mental organism.'

CHAPTER 4

Yatra and Sri Yantra

'Connection is why we're here; it is what gives purpose and meaning to our lives.'

—Brene Brown

In Advaita Vedanta, for any keen pupil, the point of departure lies in recognising and admitting to oneself a simple statement: I don't know that *I don't know*. A significant portion of this indefinable mystification is caused by the mind. The nature of which is 'very difficult to understand, because the mind is very subtle as well as hidden'. Undeniably, 'interiority of an individual' is a heap of complexity and confusion. Therefore, the development of the mind is paramount, because life's development means the development of the mind,' says Vedanta. According to this thought, the inquirer needs to change his outlook on life in order to fully realise himself as the Infinite Consciousness Bliss—*Satcitananda*.

na sasta na sastram na sisyo na siksa
na ca tvam na caham na cayam prapapancah I
svarupavabodho vikalpasahisnuh
tadeko 'vasistah sivah kevalo' ham II

There is no ruler nor rule, no pupil nor training.
There is no you nor I.

This universe is not, for the realisation of the true nature
Of the self does not tolerate any distinction.
That one, the residue, the auspicious, that alone, am I

—*Adi Shankaracharya,*
Dashashloki

The previous chapter dealing with Acharya's monism, establishes that the mind (*manas*) is not the knower. Adi Shankara distinguishes between *manas* that 'has doubt for its function' and *buddhi* or understanding that 'has determination for its province'. In fact, while identifying the various sense organs as instruments of perception, the mind is the 'inner instrument' or 'internal organ', hence, in Vedanta, addressed as *antahkarana*: 'The internal organ is so called because it is the seat of the functions of the senses as distinct from their outer organs. It receives and arranges what is conveyed to it through the senses. It is not itself regarded as a sense, since, if it were a sense, it could not have a direct perception of itself or its modifications' (Radhakrishnan).

The instructive *slokas* written by Adi Shankara in writings titled *Atmabodha*; *Tattvabodha*, and *Aparokshanubhuti* intensify the import regarding *antahkarana*, 'For if the mind has not attained that high intuitive subtlety, which results from assiduous practice and reflection, it will not only remain in a state of opacity, or semi-opacity, when it listens to these stanzas, but will in no time forget even the little grasp it has made of them' (S.S. Cohen).

According to Vedanta, the Mind is distinct from the body and not an integral part of the same. As the 'object of knowledge', the mind has varied functions like cognition, memory, emotion, and so on that render it as 'the seat of internal perception'. However, 'the importance of the human mind cannot be overestimated'. While it leads us to bondage, the mind is also the origin of freedom; therefore, it needs discipline. Pollutants of the mind (such as anger, greed, and hatred) disengage the individual from his/her true nature, i.e., pure consciousness—*Brahman*. Falling prey to comparison and competition, ever so frequently, makes most of us use the mind as a convenience that can effectively allow ignorance to overpower instead of enabling us to be aware. The wise confirm that Vedanta explicitly instructs that 'we are not our mind.' The need to step away from the organ of mind and experience calm is the precursor for any form of initiation directed inward.

The *Bhagavadgita*, a worthy text of Upanishadic stature, is unambiguous in its teaching that the mind alone is one's best friend and one's worst enemy. The inherent duality referred to in the scripture points to the controlled and uncontrolled mind; 'The mind is its own place, and in itself can make a heaven of hell, hell of heaven' (Milton, *Paradise Lost*). With such a gaze, Adi Shankara's idea of non-duality necessitates a 'purified mind'; that can be realised with *mantram* (for instance, OM/AUM) or *japa* (for instance, *Om Namah Shivaya*; *Hari Hi Om Tat Sat*).

digdesakaladyanapeksya sarvagam
sitadihrnnityasukham niramjanam I
yassvatmatirtham bhajate viniskriyah
sa sarvavitsarvagato'mrto bhavet II

He who renounces all activities,
worships in the sacred
And stainless shrine of Atman,
which is independent of time,
place and distance; which is present
everywhere; which is the destroyer
of heat and cold, and the other opposites;
and which is the giver of eternal happiness,
becomes all-knowing and all-pervading
and attains, hereafter, immortality. (68)

—*Adi Shankaracharya,*
Atmabodha

Explaining about Pavana (The Purifier), one of the thousand names of Vishnu, and highlighting the significance of the name of the divine, Eknath Easwaran shares, 'I can tell you from personal experience that even after repeating the *mantram* for many years, I still find more opportunitics for repeating it. With the *mantram*, you can use every bit and piece of spare time for spiritual growth.'

Grappling with tremendous uncertainty, post-Vedic India proved to be a testing ground for examining Adi Shankara's Advaita closely. It failed to fall into *a* category despite its 'wise agnosticism'. Yet, its greatest exponent 'taught us to love truth, respect reason, and realise the purpose of life'. During Shankara's time, a popular issue for *shastrartha* (debate) circuiting the philosophical and religious congregations was the power ranking between *karma marg* and *jnana marg*; the Mimansaka versus the Vedantic.

The individual seeking spiritual freedom seemed to oscillate between the choice of remaining a 'householder' or becoming a 'hermit'. With Adi Shankar's principle of non-duality, an aspirant became aware of the power of *bhakti* as well as the ethics of *karma*. It was an approach that every individual inclined to know himself or herself could avail, especially in the absence of the 'Brahmanical elite'.

In the essay 'Introduction to the Karmic Faiths' in the book *I Am Divine. So Are You,* the acclaimed mythologist Devdutt Pattanaik writes, 'every human being seeks wealth and power (*artha*) and sensual pleasures (*kama*) and liberation from karmic burdens (*moksha*), but what binds humans to others is *dharma*, that is the cornerstone of relationships. In Hinduism, as a spiritual philosophy and religion, 'the foundation of spiritual life is in *dharma*' (ethical/righteousness).

Further, the axiomatic formula intrinsic to good living is when *dharma* dictates *karma*; the outcome is naturally for the well-being of *jiva*. 'As the sun reveals all *arthas* or objects of the world, Sankara reveals the Truth (*artha*) of the Spirit for mankind,' writes Madhavacharya in his *Sankara Digvijaya*. In keeping with this understanding, this section of the chapter focuses on the importance of Adi Shankara's travels and the relevance of the *Sri Chakra* or *Sri Yantra* within the fold of his Advaita Vedanta.

It is said that the thinker in Adi Shankara existed even when he was a child. His love for knowledge and learning, but not possession of it, is indicative of his thinking, particularly in the context of his travels. When he was hardly an adolescent, Shankara embarked on an expansive and arduous voyage, enthused with the spiritual rigour that echoed '*shiva gyana, jeevan gyana*'. As an ascetic who sought *vaada-bhiksha* (an offering of philosophical augmentation), he walked the vast land, engaged in *shastratha* (debate) while acquiring a first-hand experience of its rich culture and diverse ethnicity.

Sources for the Great Master's spiritual mission include biographies (*Sankara-vijayas*), *stotra* literature, temple traditions, and a host of independent writings by Advaitins and scholars of philosophy. Amongst the ten noteworthy biographies written on Adi Shankara, the popular one is *Sankara Digvijaya* by Madhavacharya. Later, he headed the Sringeri Sharda Pettham as its 12th Shankaracharya (1380–1386).

Both the abstract idea of oneness reflected in the *Sri Yantra* and the *Yatra* undertaken to spread the same are crucial to the understanding of Adi Shankara's thought of non-duality. His talent for learning, combined with a non-conforming disposition, bears testimony to the fact that his short spanned life of thirty-two years was intended to be a benchmark, rarely accomplished by another. Such capabilities deserve an attention that is not blindfolded by belief or faith but viewed with reason.

For an entwined subject (like Adi Shankara and his idea of Advaita), a dispassionate and intelligent vision that overlooks 'fancifulness, unreliability, absence of chronological sense', is essential. Hyped in most of the biographical writings is Shankara's 'intense spirit of renunciation' that led him to attain 'spiritual endowments', and became the foundational qualifications of his concept of non-duality.

It is interesting to observe that the most frequently depicted image of Adi Shankara as *balaka bhikshu* (boy mendicant), wearing the traditional unicoloured ochre unstitched '*kasaya*' with a staff in his left hand, encapsulates the dramatic departure he made from his ancestral village, Kalady. An esoteric perspective of such a compelling visual does make a statement for anyone interested in the saga of his *digvijaya* ('conquest of the various quarters').

In pursuit of a guru, the boy renouncer began his travels from the Southern Peninsula towards the north in the direction of the undulating Vindhyas. He 'passed through various lands, and whatever he saw on the way—forest, rivers, cities, countryside, mountains, animals, men, and the rest—he looked upon as a great magic show put up by the Cosmic Magician, the Sat-cit-ananda, for His sport'. While commentator Madhavacharya's description apparently glorifies the ascetic boy (*balaka bhikshu*) Shankara, at the same time, it is indicative of him being one of the last representatives of Advaita Vedanta.

Given that the young Shankara was an extraordinary Vedantic monk, his mentor, Govindapada, was of high repute as well. 'Govinda Bhagavatapada, whose name suggests Vaishnava roots, was deeply influenced by Buddhism.' The books titled *Yogataravali*, *Advaitanubhuti*, *Brahmamrta-varsini*, and *Rasahrdayam* are said to have been Govindapada's cerebral contribution towards the study of Advaita Vedanta.

Govindapada was the son and disciple of the staunch non-dualist, Gaudapada, whom Shankara fondly refers to as '*dada guru*'; author of the *Karika* (commentary) that is 'an attempt to combine in one whole the negative logic of the *Madhyamikas* with the positive idealism of the *Upanishads*'. Gaudapada was certainly one of the earliest philosophers of the Vedic tradition who gave an impetus to Advaita Vedanta. His *Mandukya Karika* is probably the first regular thesis on the subject. According to him, *Brahman* is the only Reality. All else is an illusion. However, 'In Gaudapada, the negative tendency is more prominent than the positive. In Sankara, we have a more balanced outlook' (Radhakrishnan).

The places visited by Adi Shankara during his *Yatra* are relevant for one reason or another; however, some of the locations are considered more so than the rest. The ancient city of Omkareshwar is one such destination. Rewinding to more than a thousand years, one can only imagine a *balaka bhikshu* striding across the lush green 'island hill' nestled amidst the sparkling waters of the Narmada and its tributary, the Rewa.

Tradition records the pious environment of the Narmada valley as a favoured place for the spiritually inclined. The magnificence of the river that flows from east to west enjoys puritanical historicity by being the sole water system that has temples standing on both banks, hence also called '*Ubhay Tat Tirtha*'. The river's mystic nature is borne out etymologically as well, with the confluence of male (*nar*) and female (*mada*) in its name; indicative of the Shiva-Shakti amalgam interpreted as *Ardhanarishwar.*

The celebrated antiquity of Omkareshwar as a place of pilgrimage existed prior to Shankara's arrival. For instance, the presence of one of the twelve *svayambhu* (self-manifested) *jyotirlingas* enhances its sanctity. The momentous cave-meeting between Govidapada and Adi Shankara finds elaborate mention in the sources detailing the boy ascetic's travels. As does the historic episode of Narmada's fury, causing unprecedented flooding that subsided with Shankara's intervention. Madhavacharya writes in *Sankara Digvijaya*, 'Seeing that his teacher was absorbed in *samadhi*, he waited for a while watching the situation. Then, uttering a powerful *mantra*, he gathered all the flood waters into his water vessel, as Agastya in days of yore confined the waters of the ocean in the hollow of his palm.'

sariram surupam sada rogamuktam yasascaru
citram dhanam merutulyam I

manascenna lagnam guroranghripadme tatah
kim tatah kim tatah kim tatah kim II

Though your body be comely and remain
in perfect health, though your name be unsullied
and mountain high your hoarded gold,
yet if the mind be not absorbed in the guru's lotus feet,
what will it all avail you? What, indeed will it all avail?

—*Adi Shankaracharya,*
Guru Ashtakam

It was at Govidpada's gurukul that Adi Shankara realised the vital lesson of service to humanity as well as the need for institutionalised schools of Advaitic philosophy. The idea of the four *matthas* or *peetha-s* was conceived at Omarkareshwar. Strictly opposed to the ritualistic practices (*karmakanda*) popularised by the *mimamsakas*, Shankara understood the need for enshrining selfless service in the commune(s). Legend says it was at the bank of the River Tungabhadra at Sringeri that the incident of a hooded cobra shading a pregnant frog took place. Equating the sight of a predator protecting its prey, Adi Shankara found the location to be an ideal seat of learning. Thus, the first *peetha* or *mattha* among the four he institutionalised in different directions of the country was established.

As to the kind of initiation Shankara received at Omkareshwar, there is an air of unconventionality. Space felt in the lightless confines of a natural chamber like a cave, spiritually deconstructs the mind-body framework. The illumination of intuitive knowledge, thereby experienced by a seeker, forms the basis of his spiritual ordeal. At Omkareshwar, the sketched 'contemplative enquiry' with regard to the child prodigy (Shankara) was different.

Legend has it that both guru and disciple started 'the day with a visit to the nearby *jyotirlinga*'. Madhavacharya confirms in his chronicle,

'Sankara was victorious over the fortification of eight citadels (the *jiva*-hood constituted of the five *paranas*, the five organs of knowledge, the five organs of action, the mind with its four aspects, ignorance or *avidya*, desire or *kama*, works or *karma*, and the tendencies or *vasana*). He had no *sauvarna-dharma* (the dharmas relating to the four *varnas*); he was no *purusa-phalesu* (one attached to fruits of actions); he was also no *parthiva-ratha* (one with a sense of being identified with this body made of earth).'

Making choices and taking decisions is significantly connected with key aspects of *kaal* (time), *paatra* (individual), and *sthana* (place). Adi Shankara's travels do seek introspection, keeping these three characteristics in mind.

On Govindapada's command, Adi Shankara left for Varanasi-Kashi with the assigned task, 'to clarify the essential spiritual truths revealed by the *Vedas* through your writings and preachings' (*Sankara Digvijaya*). Popularly known as the city of Shiva, Varanasi is known to have provided Shankara with remarkable incidents. The ancient *ghats* of Varanasi witness an elegant transformation of Adi Shankara from an awakened ascetic to the enlightened Acharya, Author, and the Advaitin.

Varanasi's ancient name, Kashi, signifies 'where the cosmic light concentrates in a circle'. From its coveted mention in the scriptures to being famous as the facilitating *sthana* for the *deha mukti* (demise), the city enjoys incomparable prestige. Embedded with shrines, the place of pride is Kashi's Vishvanath temple, dedicated to Shiva; the *garbgriha* (sanctum) has one of the twelve oldest Shivalingas found in India. In addition, the presence of the River Ganga as the city's divine lifeline enhances its status exponentially. 'Better were it to be a fish or tortoise in thy waters, or a feeble lizard upon Thy banks, or a poor dog eater within two *kilometres* of Thy stream, than to be a noble king and yet far away from Thee' (John Woodroffe).

Kashi is widely acknowledged as *the* spiritual terminus. The fact that it is the second halt on Adi Shankara's route is perhaps providentially germane to the noteworthy occurrences that take place at Kashi. One day, returning after completing his regimen at the *ghat*s, Shankara encountered a chandala, 'keeper of the crematorium, the most polluted of professions in the Hindu caste hierarchy'. Seeking passage, he is supposed to have instructed the chandala to 'move aside', only for the outcaste to retort, 'My body, or my soul, the form, or the formless, the limited, or the limitless?'

Instantaneously, Shankara 'exclaimed that anyone who sees *Brahman* as the sole reality and recognises the *Atman* as the same in all is worthy of respect. All other distinctions are false' (Pavan Varma).

Acknowledging the chandala as his guru, Adi Shankara is said to have composed impromptu the *Manishapanchakam*. Each of the five verses of this collection concludes with the affirmation of non-duality over the insignificance of created dualities.

brahmaivahamidam jagacca sakalam cinmatravistaritam
sarvam caitadvaidyaya trigunaya'sesam maya kalpitam I
ittham yasya drdha matih sukhatare nitye pare nirmale
candalo'stu sat u dvijo'stu gururityesa mansa mama II 2 II

I am Brahman alone. And, this entire world
has been spread out by pure consciousness.
All this, without residue, has been superimposed
by me through nescience
Which consist of the three gunas {sattva, rajas, and tamas}.
Thus, he in whom there is firm knowledge
In respect of the eternal, blemishless supreme
{Brahman} which is unexcellable bliss,
Is the preceptor, be he a chandala or a Brahmin.
This is my conclusive view.

—*Manishapanchakam, verse 2*

Another historic episode at Varanasi narrates about Adi Shankara's lack of tolerance for ineffective means of learning. Utterly exasperated with a random student's memorising by rote the rules of Sanskrit grammar, He is said to have instantly rendered the famous *Bhaja Govindam* hymn. Each verse of the poem concludes with an exclamation aimed at awakening the unwise (*mudhamate*) aspirant from the stupor of *avidya*. Through the composition, Shankara emphasises that 'transformation helps in the glorification, spiritualisation, and integralisation' of *jiva*, which is not apart from Pure Consciousness (*Brahman*).

The essence of *Bhaja Govindam* conveys surrender to the Supreme through selfless bhakti, as that redeems the devotee in his final hour of departure. From abstract oneness (*Nirguna Brahman*), Adi Shankara leaps forth the iconic presence of personalised devotion to a God (*Saguna Brahman*), thereby emphasising that 'Hinduism is not a "religion" in the usual sense. It is a civilisation based on a simple metaphysical insight about the unity of the individual and the universe and has self-development as its objective' (Gurcharan Das).

The following two verses highlight the *bhakti-bhava* reflective of Advaita that Shankara is said to have discoursed during his stay at Kashi:

bhaja govindam bhaja govindam, govindam bhaja mudhamate I
samprapte sannihite kale, nahi nahi raksati dukrnkarane II

Worship Govinda, Worship Govinda,
Worship Govinda, O foolish one!
Rules of grammar profit nothing,
once the hour of death draws nigh.

—*Adi Shankaracharya,*
Bhaja Govindam

mudha jahihi dhanagamatrsnam kuru sadbuddhim manasi vitrsnam I

yallabhase nija-karmopattamvittam tena vinodaya cittam II

Renounce! O fool, your ceaseless thirst for hoarding gold and precious gems;
Content yourself with what may come through deeds performed in earlier lives;
Devote your mind to righteousness and let dispassion be your law.

—*Adi Shankaracharya,*
Dwadashapanjarika Stotra 1

Moksapuri, as Madhavacharya refers to Varanasi, is also the meeting place where Sanandana, the first disciple of Adi Shankara, sought his guru and thereafter was renamed as Padmapada. This student plays an important role in his teacher's life, apart from the time when he rescued his Acharya from a Kapali (Tantric). While journeying with the guru, Padmapada wrote a commentary on Adi Shankara's *Brahma Sutra Bhasya*, which is regarded as deeply insightful for understanding the Acharya's monism.

It is relevant to understand that at the time of Adi Shankara's residency, Kashi was a mosaic of spiritual, philosophical, and religious attitudes. Along with the Shaivites and Vaishnavites, as mentioned in the previous section, there were multiple theistic sects promoting their own agenda. There was nihilism of the *Madhyamika* and Yogacharya Buddhists desperately trying to salvage their lost hiatus. Following closely were the Jain *munis* with their idea of absolute pacifism in direct opposition to the *purva mimamsakas* promoting Vedic ritualism. In addition were the pluralists or *nyaya-vaisesikas* (school of logicians); the *sankhyas* advocating their *kaivalya* or aloofness; the *patanjalas* promoting yoga to control the *prana*; the *charvakas* convincing through *bhutas* (body's five elements) and the occult of the *tantrics*, predominant in Bengal and its neighbouring region. Amidst such over-crowding, Adi Shankara, with his dialectics, made his presence felt in the prominent debates and discourses held at the time.

An overview of Adi Shankara's residency at Varanasi shows that a great deal was accomplished. It proved to be an ideal location for his literary pursuits as he wrote the magnum opus, separate commentaries on the 'three canonical texts' known as *Prasthana Traya*—the *Brahma Sutra*, the *Bhagavadgita*, and the *Upanishads*. It would not be an exaggeration, thus, to state that the key factors of time (*kaal*), person (*paatra*), and place (*sthana*) did influence Adi Shankara's stay at Varanasi, exponentially.

> *sarvam vastu bhayanvitam bhuvi nram vairagyamevabhayam*
>
> Everything in this life is fraught with fear. It is renunciation alone that makes one fearless: *Vairagyasataka*
>
> —*Swami Vivekananda*

While viewing Adi Shankara's *Yatra*, it is pertinent to reflect upon the fact that 'great thinkers appear in all great ages, and are as much the creatures as they are creators of their era', and Shankara was no exception. For this reason alone, the knowledge of his life's experience enhances his ability to sense the need for an integrated system of thinking instead of rendering it as an ideology meant exclusively for the intellectual elite.

Like several other disagreements about his life, there are those concerning the route Adi Shankara took and the halts made during his *Yatra*. For instance, according to some scholars, he left Kashi for the higher altitudes with an 'assigned mission' to script commentaries, his *bhashya-s* in the serenity of the majestic Himalayas. While there are those who confirm that his residency in Kashi lasted a couple of years, during which time he visited Badarinath and wrote a great many texts while stationed there, he 'would certainly have trekked there to pay homage to Mother Ganga'. The '*Ganga Stotra*' is one of Adi Shankara's most popular poetic writings.

For a seeker, 'reverence to nature' forms an integral experience in matters of spiritual pursuits. Laxmikanta Pandhi, in his essay, 'Advaita Vedanta and Environmental Ethics' observes:

The nature of the self includes all lesser forms of existence. The universe, though it appears to be merely symbolic or *pratibhasika*, is actually *paramarthika* or Divine Consciousness itself. Thus, it can be said that Advaita Vedānta tradition has an ecological conscience as it proposes an essential unity of all existence in God, which promotes a sense of identity and empathy with the natural world.

Similar to the importance of time, person, and place, there exists a deep connection between *paatra* (person) and *pani* (water). Across the corridors of time, 'the river itself is a source of inspiration to withstand its ferocity and harsh treatment that it meted out to its residents. People worshipped the river because of its destructive power, but equally reaped benefits from it. It often played a significant role in shaping and changing the course of human actions' (Arupjyoti Saikia). In the initial phase of his journey, it is interesting to observe that Adi Shankara's documented stays were at places located on the banks of a prominent water system or in the vicinity of one. He was aware that such cities enjoyed the reputation of being popular centres of learning and were occasionally perceived as a stronghold of a particular kind of thinking.

There is a mountain of truth in the statement, 'tranquillity escapes us as long as we shun knowledge' (Pattanaik). More than fourteen hundred years ago, with Advaita, Adi Shankara recognised the verity of this overpowering observation. Discovering the intrinsic complexities on his travels across the geographical expanse of the land, he understood that its multiplicity required spiritual borrowing.

Aware that his life and work were seamlessly integrated, Adi Shankara persevered to provide a similar cohesion in his thought. His *jnana marg*, an aggregate of exceptional instructions taken from established philosophies under the aegis of the Upanishadic *Mahavakyas*, directed the misdirected. He appreciated 'how stories and songs connect with the people and create the highway to an expanded vision of life'.

Sources indicate that after his salutations at Gomukh, the source of River Ganga, Shankara 'found the idol of Narayana in the bed of the Alakananada River'; he sanctified Badari Narayana (synonymous names of Vishnu) in a cave near the hot sulphur springs. The incident exhibits an empathetic savant whose body of work deserves an engagement of the Mind, Body, and *Atman*.

The following verse clarifies the idea:

yam na santam na casantam, nasrutam na bahusrutam
na suvrttam na durvrttam veda kascit sa brahmanah.
gudhadharmasrito vidvan ajnatacaritam caret
andhavaj jadavac capi mukavac ca mahim caret.

Whom no one knows as high nore lowly born,
No one as erudite, not yet not erudite,
No one as of good deeds, not of evil deeds,
He is Brahmana in very truth.
Given up to hidden duties well fulfilled,
In secrecy let all his life be spent;
As he were blind and deaf, of sense bereft,
Thus let the truly wise pass through the world.

—*Sankara.Bhasya., iii.4.50*

Awakened to the reality that 'it is not the end of the voyage that matters but the voyage itself', leaving the meditative abode of the Himalayas, Adi Shankara directed his walkathon towards Prayaga (Allahabad). Famous for the *Triveni Sangam*—where the Ganga, the Yamuna, and the 'hidden' Saraswati flow together, it is said that he and his disciples bathed in the sacred waters.

At this point of his spiritual sojourn, Adi Shankara remained focused on establishing his intuitive knowledge experience of non-duality amongst the general public. From composing commentaries to convincing his opponents through *shastrath,* henceforth, the visit to Prayaga is with anticipation for one such debate with Kumarila Bhatta, 'reputed to be a great champion of Hinduism'. Aware of Bhatta's fame, Shankara was keen on the meeting that, in some scholars' view, may not have occurred at all. Nevertheless, *Sankara Digvijaya* provides an account wherein Kumarila Bhatta's act of redemption through self-immolation and the latter's admittance to wrongdoing is witnessed by Adi Shankara. Madhavacharya scripts the episode as:

I linked the validity of the Veda with my life. Because I used the conditional 'if', expressive of doubt, and because I learnt Buddhist scriptures by deception, I lost one of my eyes in the fall as a punishment for these two sinful acts of mine.

Hypothetically, from an exclusively ideological standpoint, had the proposed *shastrath* happened, the calibre of arguments between an emerging Advaitin and an acknowledged *karmakandin* would be truly insightful and reflective of the scholarly terrain of Indian Philosophy prevalent in medieval India. Subsequently, Adi Shankara left Prayaga for Mahishmati to meet Mandana Misra, a worthy disciple of Bhatta and 'the champion of the gospel of ritualistic works'. Chroniclers state that Shankara was assigned the task to defeat the *Mimamsaka*, 'for the establishment of the doctrines of Advaita as the true Vedic teaching'.

Located in central India, the prestige of Mahishmati as a flourishing ancient city finds mention in the classical poet Kalidasa's *Raghuvansam*, describing the special provinces of the time as, 'the palm-lined beaches and elephants of Kalinga, the gardens of Brindavan and Ujjain, the cool breeze from the Western Ghats, the charming waves of River Narmada in Mahismati, the dark waters of River Yamuna in Mathura.'

Today, Mahishmati, the celebrated ancient venue of an epic *shastrartha* between Adi Shankara and Mandana, is embroiled in controversy regarding its exact location. However, the episode at Mahishi remains significant because it goes beyond being a mere display of cerebral might between great minds with opposing sets of convictions. The incident overlooks convention with regard to social norms and is a telling statement about women and their participation in matters of higher thinking in ancient India. It is another example of Shankara's non-conformist approach while working towards a larger goal, which was to affirm the influence of thought over rites, especially in an environment where dualism reigned supreme.

Apparently, legend has it that at the entrance of Mandana's house, caged parrots were known to discuss abstruse concerns related to the validity of the *Vedas*, theory of Karma, nature of the world, and so on; an indication of the intellectual prowess of the 'Pandit of Mahishi'.

The meeting described at length in sources begins with Adi Shankara's unceremonious welcome at Mandana's house while the latter is conducting the customary rites on his father's death anniversary. The householder is visibly perturbed to see the uninvited hermit at his doorstep. On learning that the unexpected visitor was interested in '*vaada-bhiksha*, an offering of philosophic disputation', Misra agreed to the proposed debate. The rules of engagement included that 'the wager in the disputation' was the intellectual subjugation of the defeated contestant becoming the victor's disciple, indicative of Adi Shankara's steadfast intent of spreading liberation through Vedantic knowledge. Regarding the selection of an arbiter for the debate, Shankara suggested that Misra's wife, Ubhaya Bharati, assume the coveted responsibility.

It can only be assumed that the decision surprised Mandana Misra immensely, as well as enlightened him about his adversary extraordinaire. More importantly, it reiterated Adi Shankara's conviction on Vedanta *jnana* that upholds the wisdom of the scriptures that confirm, '*stree mullam dharma iti*', meaning, 'with women only *dharma* is possible'. Shankara's Advaita clearly states that the routine performance of one's duties (read *dharma*) brings one closer to Self-realisation if these are conducted with earnest intention.

In the ancient past, society did not particularly encourage women to perform *mantra uccharana* (scriptural chants). Moreover, their participation in affairs outside the house was not an accepted norm. This is why the exception made with Ubhaya Bharati validates Adi Shankara's position regarding the status of women at the time. In addition, it is also evident from his voluminous writings, particularly the *stotra sahitya*, wherein he exalts the mundane existence of a housebound woman in her multi-dimensional roles, highlighting the sense of sacrifice and unconditional affection in the performance of her duties.

The long-drawn challenge between Mandana Misra and Adi Shankara did not conclude with the latter's articulation of *jnana kanda* superseding the former's defence of *karma kanda*. The arbiter, Ubhaya Bharati, furthered it by asking Acharya to engage in a separate debate with her in order to attain an undisputed victory. Despite his complete unfamiliarity with the subject of intimate desires (*Kamasutra*), Adi Shankara accepted the challenge, seeking a month-long period for preparation.

The popular tale recounts that Shankara's yogic powers allowed him to experience the illusionary lure of *samsara* through King Amaruka's dead body, a ruler well-known for his harem of a hundred queens. On his return, not only did he win the debate with Ubhaya Bharati, but the 'educational' interim envisioned Adi Shankara to compose an abundance of *stotras* (hymns) devoted to the insurmountable Shakti (Sakta), the Mother Goddess.

> *sivah saktya yukto yadi bhavati saktah prabhavitum*
> *na cedevam devo na khalu kusalah spanditum api.*
>
> Shiva, when he is united with Shakti, is able to create;
> otherwise he is unable even to move
>
> —*Adi Shankaracharya,*
> *Saundaryalahri, verse 1.*

Madhavacharya devotes an entire chapter in *Sankara Digvijaya*, detailing the course of the high-profile event, who asked what, and so on. However, a highlight of this episode was that the Vedic ritualism lost its mantle of dominance to the prestige of the scriptural epistemology. Adi Shankara's grasp of the Veda-Vedanta and his skilful interpretation restored the doctrine fundamental to the Hindu belief system. It would be accurate to say that 'Hinduism has always valued the *Veda*, but while Western academicians look upon this as a book, Hindus have used it in the sense of an idea, communicated through chants, rituals, symbols, stories, songs, architecture, and music' (Pattanaik).

Another equally important outcome of the celebrated debate with Mandana Misra is the concept of shakti (the primordial energy) that emerges as a consequence of Ubhaya Bharati's participation in the extended *shastrartha.* 'All sounds and therefore movements form the "Garland of Letters", which is worn by the Divine Mother, from whose aspect as *Om* or the General Sound (*Samanya-spanda*) of the first creative movement of all particular sounds and things come, for all things may be rendered in terms of sound' (Woodroffe). In the course of his travels, Adi Shankara's temple visits substantiate that his Advaita did embrace *Devi puja* (worshipping the Goddess), both in image and the abstract representation as *Sri Yantra* (also known as *Sri Chakra*).

citabhasmalepo garalamasanam dikpatadharo
jatadhari kanthe bhujagapatihari pasupatih I
kapali bhuteso bhajati jagadisaikapadavim
bhavani tvatpanigrahanaparipatiphalamidam II

Only by taking thee for spouse did
Shiva become the unrivalled Lord
He who is naked and uncouth,
besmeared with ash from the funeral pyre;
Whose hair is matted on his head,
about whose neck are venomous snakes
The Lord of every living thing.

—*Adi Shankaracharya,*
Devyaparadhakshamapana Stotra

It is said that during the course of his long stay at Sringeri, Adi Shankara wrote extensively, including some of his famous *Prakarna Granthas*, namely, *Vivekcudamani, Atma Bodha, Aparokshanubhuti*, and *Sarva-Vedanta-sara-samgraha.* His disciple, Suresvara (formerly Mandana Misra), was appointed the Sringeri *peetha's* foundational head responsible for imparting the wisdom of the *Yajur Veda.* As a devotional *sthana*, the temple's presiding deity had to be the Goddess of Knowledge, Saraswati, also known as Sharada. The *Mahavakya* (Upanishadic declaration) '*Aham brahm asmi*' from the *Brhadaranyaka* Upanishad is the instruction for the Dasnami *sanyasis* bearing the titles *Sarasvati, Bharati*, or *Puri.*

Some believe that the prestige of the Sringeri temple is actually accorded to Mandana Misra's wife, Ubhaya Bharati, also called Sharada Devi (an incarnation of Goddess Saraswati), who is responsible for Adi Shankara acquiring knowledge of *devi* shakti.

katakse dayardram kare jnanamudram
kalabhirvinidram kalapaih subhdram I
purastrim vinidram purastungabhadram
bhaje saradambamajasram madambam II

I constantly worship my Mother, Sharadamba.
Her side glances are moist with compassion.
She shows the gesture of knowledge by her hand.
She has the efflorescence of different arts.
She looks very auspicious with her necklace of pearls.
She is the foremost among women. She is fully awake.
She has the {river}Tungabhadra {flowing} in her front.

—*Adi Shankaracharya,*
Sarada Bhujanga Prayatastakam

After establishing the first *mattha* (*peetha*), a temple for Goddess Sharada and consecrating the *Sri Yantra* at Sringeri, entrusting his four devoted students namely, Padmapada, Suresvara, Hastamalaka, and Totaka with his work, Adi Shankara is said to have left for Kaladi, to see his mother, Aryamba, who, apparently, was on her death-bed, honouring the promise he had made to her at the time Shankara embarked on his *Yatra*. In keeping with his unorthodox disposition, the devoted son fulfilled his mother's wish of performing the last rites despite being a *sanyasin*. Tradition narrates that to ease Aryamba's physical pain, he composed impromptu the *Shiva bhujangam* and *Vishnu bhujangam*, seeking divine intervention for his mother's peaceful end.

Facing stiff opposition and hostility from his relatives in the village, Adi Shankara single-handedly conducted the cremation in the compound of his house; another instance of his departure from convention. Thereafter, he left for Sringeri, where the four loyal pupils were waiting in anticipation for their Acharya to continue with his 'spiritual odessey'.

Viewed by some scholars as the second phase of his *Yatra*, Adi Shankara's travel henceforth is that of an acknowledged Master of Advaita, advocating non-duality, inclusive of devotion (*bhakti*), and knowledge (*jnana*). In fact, Vedanta affirms that a philosopher can be a devotee and vice versa. Poet Shankara's *Sivanandalahri,* verse 61, illuminates the *bhakti-jnana* coalesce with five different examples, validating the core idea elegantly:

ankolam nija-bija santatir ayaskantopalam sucika
sadhvi naija-vibhum lata ksitiruham sindhuh saridvallabham I
prapnotiha yatha tatha pasupateh padaravindadvayam
cetovrttir upetya tisthati sada sa bhaktir ity ucyate II

That state of mind is called bhakti or divine love,
wherein all movements of thought go automatically
to the lotus feet of the Lord and stick forever,
just as the seeds of the anglola tree gravitate to
the parent tree, the iron needle to the magnate bar,
the devoted wife to her husband,
the creeper to the tree and river to the ocean.

It is particularly significant to understand that Adi Shankara's experiences (during his *Yatra*) showed him the way to propagate the effectiveness of *upasana* (worship) for Self-realisation. His wide range of eulogies extolling the divinity validates his conviction. Nonetheless, the core of his instruction remains entrenched in the truth that *Brahman* is the only Reality and can be realised through the three gateways of: *sruti* (Scriptures); *yukti* or *tarka* (reasoning), and *anubhava* (intuition).

In the ancient art of teaching epistemology, the eloquence of the teacher is not the only reason for the imparting to be effective; the weight of what is being taught is of considerable importance. Through his observations, Acharya Shankara was partaking the fact 'that in social contexts involving diversity, living together well across differences is aided by accurate and comprehensive knowledge of one another'. The institutionalisation of Shankara's Advaita during his *Yatra* seeks a similar understanding.

From Sringeri, Acharya Shankara, along with his favoured four disciples, directed his *Yatra* eastwards to Puri, in the vicinity of Mahodadhi Tirtha (Bay of Bengal), where he initiated the Govardhan Matha and appointed disciple Hastamalaka as the pontiff responsible for imparting the *Rig Veda.*

The presiding divinities of the *peetha* are Jagannath and Purshottama with Goddess Shakti as Vrsala Vimala. The *Mahavakya* '*Prajnanam brahma*' from *Aitareya* Upanishad is the Vedantic pointer to meditate upon for the Dasnami *sanyasis* with order titles of *Vana* and *Aranya*.

Impassioned with a vision for a spiritually unified geographical realm, Adi Shankara left Puri, bound westward for Dwarka (Gujarat) in order to establish the Kalika Matha that is blessed with the waters of the River Gomati. His disciple, Padmapada, was made in charge of the dissemination of the *Sama Veda*. The ruling divinities are Siddhleshwara with Goddess Shakti as Bhadra Kali. The ascetics of the Dasanami titles *Tirtha* and *Asrama* seek their guidance from the *Chandogya* Upanishad *Mahavakya,* '*Tat Tvam Asi*'.

The last of the *peethas* founded by Adi Shankara was the Jyotir Matha in the North, at Badrikashrama. He entrusted the charge to his pupil Totaka, who was responsible for spreading the knowledge of the *Atharva Veda*. In the proximity of the River Alakananda, the shrine's sanctum has Lord Narayana with Goddess Purnagiri. The *Mandukya* Upanishad *Mahavakya,* '*Ayum atma brahm*', illuminates the path of the Dasnami ascetics bearing the titles *Giri*, *Parvata*, and *Sagara*.

In order to keep the flame of Veda-Vedanta *jnana* alive and the need to interact with the people, each of the foundational pontiffs was instructed by Adi Shankara to travel to different parts of the land rather than rendering the *peetha* into seats of uncontrolled power. The Acharya's pragmatism dictated that, as heads of these orders, it was their duty from time to time to be aware of the spiritual pulse of the people as well as to examine the ground reality of their teachings. Thus, the officiating priests were meant to be the spiritual emissaries representing diversity while involved in the exchange of ideas within the contoured land. To ensure the effective functioning of the centres, Adi Shankara is supposed to have dictated a rulebook, *Mahanusasanam*, to King Sudhavana of Gujarat.

Abiding by Acharya Shankara's dictum, it is said that even today, priests at Orissa *mattha* officiate at Dwarka *peetha,* while the Pandas at the Puri belong to Gujarat. Similarly, at the Badrinath temple, Nambudri Brahmins of Kerala, known as 'Ravals', are the officiating clergy to date. The tradition seems to be continuing in other temples, like Rameshwaram, where the priests belong to Benares or Kashmir. In a similar manner, interconnecting the *matthas* with the *Dashanami Sampradaya* suggests the iconic Advaitin's vision for a spiritually unified country.

For maintaining the sanctity of the text-in-hand, controversy regarding Kanchi as the fifth *mattha* founded or not by Acharya, as well as the debate regarding it being Adi Shankara's place of rest, has been deliberately avoided by the author.

Over a passage of time, the re-telling of Adi Shankara's *Yatra* by different chroniclers reads differently for obvious reasons. For instance, details of his itinerary are confusing, especially in the absence of chronological markings. While Shankara may have travelled to many more places than have been documented, particulars furnished regarding some of the places he visited are inadequate for determining the purpose of his visit. Between omissions and exaggerations, a careful examination of available resource material is necessary.

Interestingly, throughout his *Yatra*, his interactions are not restricted to commoners; royalty also gets the opportunity to experience Adi Shankara's enigmatic persona. The strength of his thought attracted the might of kingdoms with rulers enthusiastic for his discourses; it is known that several heads of state extended their resources and patronage for propagating his notion of Advaita. For instance, King Rajasekhara of Kerala, who is supposed to have compiled texts from Acharya's verbatim delivery after the previous work, was destroyed by fire. Similarly, the ruler of Ujjain is known to have followed Adi Shankara on his travels after the Acharya is said to have visited Girinara, Somnatha, and Prabhasa in Saurashtra (Gujarat) on the king's invitation. Also, the ruler of Kashmir extended his support during Shankara's stay at Srinagar, where he is known to have composed the famous elegy, the *Saundarya Lahari.*

Adi Shankara's *Yatra* also includes a chapter about his journey in the north-western region of the country. Sources say that after passing through Srimala in Saurashtra, into Pushkara (in Rajasthan) and crossing the desert, Acharya's travel extended into the kingdom of Gandhara. He is said to have visited Purusapura, Bahlika, Kamboj, and Takshila, which were considered as strongholds of the *Madhyamakas*, before heading towards the North-East to Kamrupa (Assam), while halting at Kashmir.

Sri Yantra

The famous novelist Saumerset Maugham said, 'If you single-handedly chase pleasure, very soon you will find nothing pleasing anymore.' The core of this statement points towards the predicament we face while coping with the illusion (*maya*) called life. All beings have a natural state (*svabhava, niyati*). The creation is nothing but an outflow of the delight of the Divine; the sentiments (*rasa*) and existence on earth are permeated by this sap of life, which assumes a nine-fold form, such as *sringara*, *birya*, *karuna*, etc. These fine sentiments soon become distorted and take shape as *kama*, *krodha*, etc., with their attendant *punya* or *papa* (Krishnakumar).

According to Vedanta, the awareness that the human body is a shrine is paramount, and it commands treatment, sustenance, and maintenance in accordance. Thus, the concepts of worth and worship are not too far apart. For studying the *Sri Yantra/Sri Chakra*, the approach necessitates, 'Logically to understand the knowledge you receive and then to turn it into wisdom, to make it part of your life, it needs emotional integration' (Sri Sri Ravi Shankar).

In Sanskrit, *chakra* usually refers to a 'wheel' and its etymology indicates 'that by which anything is done' (*kriyate anena*). The instrument known as *chakra, yantra,* or *mandala* is a sphere energised by influence, a consecrated group, an arena for the play of thoughts, feelings, and forces that function both inside and outside the devotee.

Ramachandra Rao, in his *The Tantra of Sri-Chakra* (Bhavanopanishat), writes:

> Whenever the sense in which the word is employed, it invariably means a power-filled, an arrangement of parts so as to accomplish the desired end. The circular form, which the *chakra* usually brings to mind, denotes both comprehension and facility. It comprehends all the parts, units, and details in a compact and effective manner so that the whole form is unitary and functional.
>
> The imaginary idea of *chakra* as a potent pattern of forces involving cohesion, regularity, and functional unity is an old one in India. Its visual representation is to be found even in the remains of the Indus Valley civilisation.

In the *Bhakti* tradition, *Sri Yantra* has a coveted status that provides a canopy for other representations of *tantra vidya*, a realm of knowledge that symbolically intensifies the subtleties of Advaita. In response to the existential question, 'What is the cause of this universe? Is it *Brahman*?' *Svetasvatara Upanishad* states, '*Brahman* has used its own *Atma Sakti* in projecting the universe'; Adi Shankara reiterates in *Sutra Bhasya 'paramesvara saktah samast jagadvidhayanya'*.

Described as a 'psychocosmogram', that is, a heightened spiritual amalgam of the microcosm of the universe and the human body, the *Sri Yantra* is a configuration that manifests the sublime divinity. It is a talisman of wellness that is initiated using the names and forms (read *mantra*) for reaching 'the nameless, formless Supreme Being'. 'The worship of *Sakti* as the world-mother displaced Vedic ritualism. The literature relating to this phase of Hinduism is called *tantra*. It is famous for its reverence for women, who are regarded as forms of the divine mother.' As the Saptasati verse says, '*Vidyah samastas tava devi bhedah. Striyah samastah sakala jagatsu*' (xi.5).

The extent of *Sri Yantra*'s significance is evident from the expansive literature available on the diagrammatic Vedic apparatus. The earliest reference to Saktaism or Shaktism is in one of the hymns in the *Rig Veda* that describes Shakti 'as the embodiment of power, "the supporter of the earth living in heaven". She is the supreme power "by which the universe is upheld", the great mother of the devotees (suvratanam), and soon became identified with "Uma of golden hue" of the *Kena* Upanishad.'

The *Tripura* Upanishad and the *Bhavanopanishad* are devoted to the 'importance given to the worship of *Sri Yantra*' in spiritual instruction. A comprehensive study of the cosmic order through the three and nine-fold division in the mystic symbol is dealt with in the *Tripura* Upanishad, while the *Bhavanopanishad* details about 'Goddess Lalita, whose body is the complete universe, is verily one's own Self and well within reach'.

Adi Shankara's efforts to ensconce the *Sri Chakra* in temples like Kolluru and Sringeri, where *Devi puja* was dominant, needs to be understood in the context of his philosophy and not essentially as a consequence of 'episodes' with Tantric sects that are said to have occurred during his travels. Confirming Adi Shankara's assimilation of *Sri Yantra* in his instruction (of non-duality), the Shankaracharya of the Sringeri Matha opines, 'Adi Shankara has set forth worship of Devi in *Sri Chakra* form in his *Saundarya*

Lahari and *Prapanchasara*. This form of worship occupies a high place in all the mathas established by him.'

It is true that 'there is no thought without language. They may be inseparably connected as aspects of one and the same concrete, that is, actual, process, but between aspects, there is no sequence' (Woodroffe); an accurate evaluation of *Sri Yantra* being the abstract model of non-duality in Adi Shankara's matrix of Advaita.

Seeking *Saguna Brahman*, in accordance with Advaitin Shankara's thought, that is, integrating the *Brahman* ('Universal Soul') with the *Atman* ('Individual Soul'), the tools of facilitation available are as follows: (i) Gods/Goddesses; (ii) Sounds in the form of *mantras*; (iii) Diagrammatic representation, and (iv) Combination of *mantra* and Yantra which form *tantra*. His awareness regarding the potency of *Sri Yantra* as a highly sophisticated, complex, and sacred 'instrument' used for worship, devotion, and meditation is a compelling explanation for incorporating the concept of Shakti (or Sakti) in Advaita Vedanta.

In the Oxford Dictionary of Hinduism, nearly a two-page meaning of the term *tantra* while explaining *Sri Yantra* reads, 'The Sri Vidya also provides instances of other characteristic Tantric techniques such as the use of geometric figures or *Yantra* (or in other contexts *mandala*); these are accompanied by recitation of *mantras*, particularly seed (*bija*) *mantras* (the sonic form of the deity) to realise the Goddess and her power in the body of the initiate.'

Through this definition, the *Mahakarana*, or the causal force, possesses all sound and light forms; hence, the 'linear configuration' of the Divine, as opposed to the human body form attributed to them. It is these lines (of illumination) patterned in a specific diagrammatic representation that constitute the *Sri Chakra*, providing an abstract idea of devotion rather than the conventional deified reverence.

Philosophically, *Sri Yantra* represents the *paramarthik* (ontological) and the *vyavaharik* (transactional or practical). At one level, the science of the lines confines the revered object, lending it a finite form, 'while the Being is infinite'. This enables the individual's mind to perceive that which is beyond perception. At another level, the *chakra* indicates 'the sense of movement', as specified by the 'wheel-like peripheral arrangement' of the *mandala*. By this understanding, the *Sri Yantra* is an embodiment of 'both the static and dynamic components' of *Brahman*, the Supreme Being.

According to Woodroffe:

> *Sakti* is spoken of as female, that is, as Mother, because that is the aspect of the Supreme in which It is thought of as Genetrix and Nourisher of the universe. But God is neither male nor female. These are all symbolisms borrowed from the only world which we ordinarily know—that around us. In relation to non-duality, he states, 'For the *Sakta-Tantra* is the *Sadhana-sastra* of Advaitavada presenting the reaching of Vedanta in its own manner.' The *Tripura Rahasya* accentuates the *Yantra's* importance with the declaration: 'I am abstract intelligence, wherefrom the cosmos originates, whereon it flourishes, and wherein it dissolves, like images in a mirror.'

Adi Shankara's visit to Mookambika temple at Kollur (in present-day Karnataka), as described by Madhavacharya, has the *sadhaka* Shankara praising the Goddess by saying, 'These four forms of communion are: the unity of *Sri Chakra* and the six *chakras* in the body; the unity of *mantras* pertaining to the *Sri Chakra* and the six *chakras*; the unity of *Sri Chakra* and Yourself; and the unity of the *mantras* of *Sri Chakras* and Yourself. The *sadhaka* recognises all these forms of unity.' The Sharada Devi or Sri Saradamba temple at Sringeri (also in Karnataka) also has a *Sri Yantra* sculpted in rock, said to have been installed by Adi Shankara himself.

In addition to Kollur and Sringeri, during his *Yatra*, Adi Shankara facilitated the installation of the *Sri Yantra* while composing *stutis* and *stotras* at numerous temple towns that included Gokarna, Hariharapura, Sribali (Sriveli), Srisailam, Tiruvanaikkaval, Rameshwaram, Kanchipuram, Madurai, Tiruvidaimarudur, Srirangam, Kanyakumari, Tiruchendur, and Vidarbha.

Adi Shankara's temple visits and his *stotra sahitya* dedicated to Shakti during the course of his odyssey are considerable factors for the rise in his popularity across the subcontinent. In both scenarios, the common denominator is his attention to the *Yantra*; for this reason alone, he is also known by many as the *Sri Chakra Pratishtapana Acharya*—'the master who established the *Sri Chakra*'. Interestingly, his treatise, *Saundarya Lahari*, has a hundred verses expressing his utmost devotion to Shakti, and verse eleven 'explicitly pays homage to the *Sri Chakra*'.

caturbhih srikanthaih sivayuvatibhih pancabhirapi
prabhinnabhih sambhornavabhirapi mulaprakritibhih I
catuscatvarimsadvasudalakalasratrivalaya-
trirekhabhih sardham tava saranakonah parinatah II

Oh! Supreme power, your angles of abode become
forty-four in number with four wheels of auspiciousness,
Five different wheels of power, nine basic roots of nature,
and three encircling lines encasing eight and sixteen petals.

The stress on symbolism is acute and inseparable while studying *Sri Yantra* as an auspicious, symmetrical 'holographic matrix', that echoes the hermetic view 'as above so below'. Krishnakumar, in *The Sri Chakra as a Symbol of the Human Body*, says:

> *Bhavanopanishad*, one of the most important Shakta Upanishads, describes the *Bhavana* meditation in which importance is given to the material body, the mind in its various gradations and the vital forces in different fields of action and their identity established with the corresponding powers (*Shakti*) located in various parts of *Sri Chakra*. The unravelling of this identity is achieved by offering these members of the human body to the powers located on the *Sri Chakra*. This is achieved by *Bhavana* or deep meditation, contemplating, step by step, the various psycho-physical parts of the human body, the corresponding powers in the *Sri Chakra*, and dwelling on their identity.

The nine interpenetrating triangles (the *navachakra*) 'denote ascending and descending energy forms depending on whether they point upward or downward'. In ascending order (*laya krama*), each of the *navachakras* has its own specific colour, designation, and deity.

They are identified as:

i. *Bhupura*—the outermost, three-lined quadrilateral.

ii. *Sodasadala padma*—the sixteen-petal lotus.

iii. *Ashtadala padma*—the eight-petal lotus.

iv. Chaturdasara—the *chakra* of fourteen triangles.

v. Bahirdasara—the *chakra* of ten outer triangles.

vi. Antardasara—the *chakra* of ten inner triangles.

vii. Ashtakona—the *chakra* of eight triangles.

viii. Bindu—the point in the centre.

It is interesting to observe that texts on *Sri Yantra* provide detailed information regarding the *navachakras* and their relationship with (i) the *tattvas* of the universe, (ii) the *varnas* (letters) of the syllabary, (iii) the *chakras* of the human body, (iv) the *tithis* (dates) of the month, and (v) the days of the year.

The apex of the triangle is indicative of the dire need of the *Atman* to merge with the *Brahman,* while the inverted triangle's nadir signifies 'the reciprocity extended' by the Supreme One-with-no-second. The four upward-facing are identified with Shiva, denoting the male principle, and the five downward-facing represent Shakti, the female principle. In addition, the 'primary triangle gradually evolves into other geometric forms, such as the square, pentagon, hexagon, octagon, and other polymorphic contours, constructing a uniquely scientific geometry that ensconces causal, vital, and physical forces with mystic dimensions.

The spiritual dynamism of the *Yantra's* diagrammatic representation is overwhelming for those who perceive Tantric philosophy or Shaktaism only as an ancient occult sect. According to *Bhavanopanishad Prayogavidhi*:

> The mediation starts from the outermost *chakra* of *Sri Chakra.* In the first line of *Bhupura* are located the siddhis viz., *animai* (minuteness), *laghima* (lightness), *mahima* (greatness), *isatva* (lordship), *vasitva* (control), *prakamya* (power to have whatever one wants), *bhukti* (enjoyment), *iccha* (desire), *prapti* (attainment), and *sarva kamasiddhi* (attainment of all desires). These are in the human complex, natural state and the nine sentiments—*sringara* (erotism), *virya* (heroism), *karuna* (compassion), *adbhuta* (wonder), *hasya* (humour), *bhayanaka* (terror), *bibhatsa* (disgust), *raudra* (wrath), and *santa* (quiescence). In the second line of the *Bhupura* are located

> *kama* (lust), *krodha* (anger), *lobha* (covetousness), *moha* (delusion), *mada* (pride), *matsarya* (envy), *punya* (merit), and *papa* (demerit).
> Located in the line of *Bhupura* are the six centres of the body (*muladhara, swadhisthana, manipura, anahata, visuddhi, ajna*), the nine *sahasras* (one above and one below), and the *indrayoni*. These nine entities are called *mudra saktis*.
> *Tantra* speaks of fourteen *nadis* viz., *alambusha, kuhuh, visvodara, varuni, jastijihva, yasovati, payasvini, gandhari, pusha, sankhini, saraswathi, ida, pingala,* and *sushumna*. These fourteen *nadis* form the fourteen powers represented in the *Chaturdasa kona*.

According to Radhakrishnan, the metaphysics of the *Yantra* interprets:

> If Siva is consciousness (cit), Sakti is the formative energy of consciousness, Cidrupini. Brahma,Visnu, and Siva perform their function of creation, preservation, and destruction in obedience to Sakti. In the perfect experience of *ananda*, Siva and Sakti are indistinguishable. The two coalesce in one being. Siva answers to the indeterminate *Brahman* in a state of quiescence; Sakti is determinate *Brahman* endowed with *iccha* (will), *jnana* (knowledge), and *kriya* (action), projecting the whole objective universe. Siva and Sakti are one, since force is inherent in existence. The force may be at rest or in action, but it exists nonetheless in both states. The potentiality of the whole object-world exists as the Sakti of Siva.

Lotus is the common motif in Shaktism, indicative of the *Atman* responding to the illumination from the Divine. The nucleus of the *Sri Chakra* is the presiding deity's space (indicated by *Bindu*), and the periphery is the gallery of the 'supplemental god forms' or *avarana devtas*. Each subordinate shakti has a separate function to perform. Hailed as the most intricate and important of all *Yantras* in *tantra shastras*, the leading deity of *Sri Chakra* is Goddess Lalita (also known as Tripurasundari), surrounded by fifteen subordinate shaktis or *Nityas*. The text *Lalita Sahasranam* is inundated with tales of glory and supremacy of the Goddess who is the controller of the three realms of power (Shakti), wealth (Lakshmi), and knowledge (Saraswati).

In *Saundarya Lahari*, the poet Adi Shankara elegantly describes the divine mother manifested as the *Sri Chakra*:

catussastya tantraih sakalamatisandhaya bhuvanam
sthitastattatsiddhiprasavaparatantraih pasupatih I
punastvannirbandhadakhilapurusarthaikaghatana
svatantram te tantram ksititalamavatitaradidam II

The Lord of creatures, having created the entire
universe with sixty-four tantras,
the chief sources of occult powers remained satisfied.
But on your insistence,
he introduced into the earth this tantra of yours,
which bestows all the four aspirations of men:
dharma, artha, kama, and moksha.

As 'the mother of all things', Shakti is distinguished as gross and subtle. She is attributed with the following five functions: (i) illumination (*abhasa*), colouration (*rakti*), examination (*vimarsana*), sowing the seed (*bijavasthana*), and lamentation (*vilapanata*). In addition, *Maya* is looked upon as the substance of Devi, ('*samyavastha gunopadhika brahmarupini devi*'). In Shaktism, the *Yantra* is the epitome of divinity and is vital to the nodal concepts of *Nada* and *Bindu*. Woodroffe explains:

These two Saktis (Nada, Bindu) are stages in the movement towards the manifestation of the Self as object, that is, as the Universe. He goes on to explain their respective attributes by saying, 'Nada is the most subtle aspect of Sabda, as the first putting forth of Kriyasakti. Paranada and Para Vak are Parasakti. Nada, into which it evolves, is the unmanifested (Avyaktatma) seed or essence (Nadamatra) of that which is later manifested as Sabda, devoid of particularities such as letters and the like (*Varnadivisesa-rahitah*). It develops into Bindu, which is of the same character. From the *Mantra* aspect, as the source of Sabda, this Mahabindu, as it differentiates to 'create' is called the Sabda-Brahman.

Usually, the Shakti schools of *Tantra,* predominantly in Kashmir, Bengal, and the North-East, are associated with two *avatars* (incarnation) of the Goddess, either 'fierce (*ugra*) or benevolent'. *Kalikula*, 'belonging to the family of the Black Goddess, originating from North-East and Northern India' or *Srikula*, 'belonging to the family of the Auspicious Goddess', originating in Kashmir and the South, notably in the *Sri Vidya* tradition.

Biographers have made specific mention of Adi Shankara's experiences (in some cases described as 'attacks') with seasoned practitioners of Sakta Tantrism during his travels, for instance, in Maharashtra, Karnataka, Bengal, and Assam. The occasional incidents with the Kapalikas strengthened Acharya Shankara's resolve to spread Advaita while simultaneously acquainting him with occult practices of the day.

The teaching on Shakti and its relation to the devotion of *Sri Chakra* is Adi Shankara's adherence to the 'rich tradition spanning millennia of ritual chants, or the discourse of the gurus, or the poetry of the Vedic sages'. Their inclusion in his instruction is reflective of the Great Master's observance and understanding of the milieu he experienced. The orbit of Adi Shankara's Advaita includes the forcefulness of Shakti, more so, in the codified temple worship wherein the metaphysical representation of the same exists as the *Sri Yantra*.

Practical Vedanta: The Three 'S's

As shared earlier as well, my yatra with this manuscript has been an undulating one. Since March 2017, when the work of writing a book on Adi Shankara and his idea of Advaita was first assigned to me, challenges have been a constant companion. From limited fieldwork to managing familial exigencies to desperately seeking a mind that can script in the absence of fear, my physical, mental, and emotional self has catapulted multiple times.

Even after the first draft of the manuscript was dispatched on 30 September 2020, spells of despair and frequent bouts of self-doubt took charge. A reworking of the self was the answer—purpose overrode achievement. October 2022 onwards, the three 'S's became the pivot to my daily living: Seva, Satsang, and Salsa; All three aligned to settle the disturbance within. Family and friends experienced the restored me in the absence of any conversation, much less confrontation and for that, am deeply grateful.

The stiff learning that arises from cathartic episodes often propels the individual towards practising a methodology that mends well. Life's reminders continue to keep a close check; an acceptance of 'Soul has ultimate knowledge' uplifts me with instruction that I mindfully choose not to forget. With Seva, Satsang, and Salsa, mindfulness is paramount; hence, the need to please or conform to norms dissolves, and the practice of knowing the real self is more apparent.

Sahitya

To Be is greater than belief, for Being is before belief. Belief is of the mind and is conceptual, whereas Beingness is the light of the Eternal.

—Mooji

Jawaharlal Nehru describes Adi Shankara as a curious mixture of a philosopher and scholar, an agnostic and a mystic, a poet and a saint, and, in addition to all this, a practical reformer and an able organiser. For the author, Adi Shankara is the epitome of spiritual instruction; the Great Master, who when questions, raises the level of an inquirer's pursuit and, with answers, delivers Advaita, with precision and without embellishments. While reflecting upon his life and work, the image conjured is that of an extraordinary talent, endowed with exceptional energy, dedicated to the service of humanity. Centuries later, Adi Shankara and his work remain topical, provoking commoners, thinkers and scientists alike. It is a rare distinction.

Identifying the urge to address experiential questions, Adi Shankara covers the spectrum of soul search through his Advaita Vedanta. More importantly, his idea of non-duality *is* the axis for the individual—*jiva,* and his liberation. For instance, explaining the phenomenon of 'I' or 'Me'-ness, the Great Master calls it a '*bhranti*' (mistake or error). Quoting the *Katho* Upanishad, he explains that from the time of birth, an individual's senses precede in an outward direction. The fact that the individual does not see (read realise) the self is a natural occurrence.

Consequently, the actions performed are of a 'mistaken identity' that originates from the individual's 'I'-ness, the 'bacteria of *aham*'; that is, insubstantial and born of ignorance. Thus, for one's well-being, the solution lies in getting rid of *aham,* but how? Shankara's response is with wisdom—*jnana* drawn from the scriptures—*sruti*, aided by reason—*yukti* or *tarka*, and realised from experience—*anubhava*. However, it is significant to remember that Vedanta's core import is that 'the reality of non-duality is not contradictory with the appearance of duality'. So, realising the Truth (about oneself) does not mean suffering, pain, etc., cease to exist. Only that being aware of one's real nature makes suffering a choice, and managing life—living—becomes less of an ordeal.

One of the most influential outcomes of Adi Shankara's spiritual travels was the vast range of literature, most of which has been interpreted by different schools and scholars worldwide. 'The many strands of the complex texture of his personality found their expression in his writings. The great point about his style is the way in which it mirrors the qualities of his mind, its force, its logic, its feeling, and its sense of humour' (Radhakrishnan).

Given the ambit of Adi Shankara's written work, it falls under three genres that define the character of the texts: *Bhasyas*—commentaries; *Prakarana-grantha-s*—pithy handbooks deconstructing the tenets of Advaita Vedanta and the *Stotras-s*—lyrical compositions dedicated to the deified divinity. However, the authentication of each and every manuscript by him remains an unsolved problem. Adi Shankara is supposed to have written about three hundred texts. More importantly, those attributed to him further compound the issue of verification. Possibly these were composed much later by those 'who bore the traditional title of Shankaracharya'.

Advaitin Shankara's *sahitya* can be systemised as the *Prasthana Traya*: *Nyaya prasthana*—the *Brahma Sutra*/*Vedanta Sutra*, *Sruti prasthana*—the *Upanishads*, and *Smriti prasthana*—the *Bhagavadgita*. Considered radical in his thinking and revolutionary in his writings, to an extent, the Great Master's word and work are misinterpreted by the prejudiced and the less informed. Viewed in isolation, Shankara's Advaita, juxtaposed with temple visits during his *Digvijaya*, is often assumed by the aforementioned as a contradiction of the non-dual principles.

Adi Shankara is classicity, far removed from hypocrisy or falsehood of any kind. It would not be an exaggeration to state that had Adi Shankara not written the commentaries (*Bhasya*) on the Vedic literature, the wisdom of these sagacious scriptures would have remained elusive. These three primordial sources form the foundation of Vedanta philosophy.

From the legendary debate with Mandana Misra, Ubhaya Bharati, Abhinavagupta, Neelkantha, to the casual interactions he had with ordinary people during his *Yatra*, Adi Shankara vigorously advocated the path of knowledge—*jnana yoga*—as the walk towards enlightenment—*Satcitananda*, emphasising that it alone liberates the individual from suffering—*dukkha*—experienced through cycles of birth and death.

In his commentary on the *Bhagavadgita,* Acharya Shankara clarifies that the genesis of action is in the mind; therefore, renunciation of the mind is critical for Self-realisation. Relying on scriptural testimony, 'What have we to do with progeny,—we who live in this region, this Self?' (*Brhadarayaka* Upanishad, iv. 4, 22), Acharya's thought—*vicara*—conjoins the *jnana yoga* and the *karma yoga* because, as he says in the *Gita-bhasya*, 'The Vedic path is twofold; one of action and the other of knowledge—*dvividho hi vedoktau dharmah pravrttilakshanau nvrtti lakshanah ca*' *(p.13).*

Staunchly opposed to the assertion that Vedic rituals alone can lead to liberation (*moksha*), the Great Master argued against the validity of such claims, thereby contesting the standpoint of the orthodox ritualists—*purva mimamsakas*. By exalting *jnana,* he did not dismiss the importance of the *Vedas* or the rituals as documented in the same. In the *Brahma Sutra Bhasya*, Adi Shankara unequivocally emphasises 'the *Veda* is eternal wisdom, and contains the timeless rules of all created existence. The *Vedas* are of superhuman origin (*apauruseya*) and express the mind of God'. Similarly, he questions the *karma-kandins* who insist that *karma marg* alone led to the ultimate freedom. His notion of Advaita disputes such claims and opposing views by proving that knowledge is the sine qua non for ultimate freedom.

brahma 'rpanam brahma havir
brahmagnau brahmana hutam
brahmai 'va tena gantavyaim
brahmakarmasamadhina

For him, the act of offering is God,
the oblation is God.
By God is it offered into the fire of God.
God is that which is to be attained by him
who realises God in his works.

—*Bhagavadgita, 4. 24.*

Brahman is the Absolute Reality. According to Adi Shankara, the reality is non-dualistic; it appears to be dual. For a basic understanding of his subtle yet deep import, in the *Gita-Bhasya* (Ch.II.46), the Acharya advances an integrated thought that allocates due positions to the divergent ideas of *Shakti*, *Bhakti*, and *Mukti*, that are otherwise mutually exclusive. It is the resonance of this concept of non-dual Vedanta that Shankara extols in all his textual works. His commentaries grasp the Upanishadic wisdom, 'the knowing that is being' (*Mundaka* Up.).

Standing between the world—*jagat*—and the transactional truth—*paramarthika sat*, Acharaya Shankara witnessed the appearance—*mithya*. He realised that the mystery (of *jagat-mithya*) must be ultimately supраrational, not conceivable or expressable by '*anirvacaniya*'—the unutterable, indescribable.

Far from being a narrow dogmatic guru or a sectarian *darshanik* or a biased theologian, Acharya Shankara's spiritual vision pivoted on *karma, bhakti*, and *jnana* for *jivan mukti*; 'The entire world of manifestation and multiplicity is not real in itself and seems to be real only for those who live in ignorance (*avidya*).'

Scanning through his commentaries, it is in the introduction section that Adi Shankara posits the context and develops the reasoning based on his 'intuitive cognisance' and grasp of the Scriptures—*sruti*—for providing an interpretation of the seminal thought of non-duality. Presenting a 'bird's eye-view', the primers of *bhasyas* are extremely relevant to the understanding of Veda-Vedanta, for establishing the singularity of thought (*ekvakyata*) that is *jiva Brahma ekam* (*Atman-Brahman* are one and the same).

In addition, the introduction(s) of his commentaries exhibit Shankara's exceptional skill in extracting wisdom from the veiled meanings of the *sutra* with remarkable precision and articulating it lucidly for maximum reach. For instance, in the introduction of his *Bhasya* on *Katha* Upanishad (1.2.4), he affirms that knowledge—*jnana*—is for a *vasishtha adhikari*, a specific person with qualifications. According to him, such an individual is usually a *sanyasin* or a *mumuksha*, as per the *nvrtti* dharma. The Great Master goes on to explain about dialects of *preyas* (worldly outlook) and *sreyas* (spiritual outlook), comparing both to darkness and light, respectively.

> There goes neither the eye, nor speech, nor mind;
> we know It not: nor do we see how to teach one about It.
> Different It is from all that are known,
> and are beyond the unknown as well—thus we have
> heard from the ancient seers who explained That to us.
>
> —*Kena Upanishad I.3.9*

It is the writings of Adi Shankara that are decisively helpful in examining the influence of Advaita Vedanta. The command of his thought asserted through the commentaries on the *Prasthana Traya* is fundamental to the subsequent interpretations developed in the recent past.

For instance, in the *Gita-Bhasya* (4.18), mentoring on *jnana yoga* and interpreting verse 18, the Acharya Shankara says: The truth that the Self is actionless, so clearly taught by *sruti*, *smriti*, and reason, has been taught here also in ii. 20–24; and it will be taught hereafter. It is, however, a deep-rooted habit of the mind to connect action with the actionless Self, though it is contrary to His real nature; wherefore, 'even the wise are deluded as to what is action and what is inaction' (v. i6). Action pertains to the physical body (*deha*), etc., but man falsely attributes action to the Self and imagines 'I am the agent, mine is action, by me shall the fruit of action be reaped'.

> *karmany akarma yah pasyed*
> *akarmani ca karma yah*
> *sa buddhiman manusyesu*
> *sa yuktah krtsnakarmakrt*
>
> He who can see inaction in action,
> Who can also see action in inaction,

he is wise among men, he is devout,
he is the performer of all action.

—*Adi Shankaracharya,*
Gita-Bhasya, 4.18.

One of the striking features of Adi Shankara's *sahitya* is the simplicity with which he illustrates the deepest concepts regarding non-duality. Especially, in his use of the Sanskrit language, it is obvious that his focus is towards clarity of content and not its ornamentation.

At the time when Sanskrit was meant to be the *lingua franca*, its misuse by the Brahmanical order rendered it a lost means of communication for the ordinary. By scripting his works in Sanskrit that is easily comprehensible, Adi Shankara disregards convention and social barriers by educating people of diverse cultural backgrounds. Thus, the Advaitin's endeavour with regard to the spread of his non-dual thought goes beyond the parameters of routine engagement for a great many people who experienced intimidation and humiliation at the hands of a language.

Conscious of the caste discrimination prevalent during his time and the consequences it had on society at large, Adi Shankara, through his writings, redressed the issue by frequently quoting the scriptures, thereby reiterating that such distinctions were created by mankind and not the divine. More importantly, he firmly dispelled the misconceptions related to the *varna-ashram*, especially in the practice of the Vedic rites as popularised by the Brahmanical order. His collection of *Bhasyas, prakarana grantha-s*, and *stotra-s*, emphasised awakening to the Absolute Truth, *Brahman*, and the individual's *Atman*, being of the One with no second. The following *sloka* from a popular treatise, *Vakya Vrtti*, echoes the same idea elegantly.

svapnajagarite supti bhavabhavau dhiyam tatha,
yo vettyavikriyah sakatso'hamityavadharaya. (22)

He am I, the one Consciousness which is
the changeless Self that is directly cognised,
that illumines the three states of waking,
dream and deep sleep; and that which
Illumines appearance and disappearance of

the intellect and its functions—
'He am I'(So'ham) – ascertain thus and realise.

For this chapter, the author has chosen an overview of selected texts considered as authentic writings of Adi Shankara—summaries of the *Brahma Sutra,* the *Mandukya* Upanishad, the *Brhadaranyaka* Upanishad, *Aparokshanubhuti*, and an assortment of *Stotras*.

Bhasya on the *Brahma Sutra*

Spiritual aspiration in the Indian tradition begins with the study of the *Sutra*, the *Sruti*, and the *Smriti.* The muted profundity of the aphorismic instruction of the *Sutra* and the *Upanishads* requires exceptional insight illumined by a seasoned intellect. Commencement of these ancients is not possible without the aid of Adi Shankara's commentaries.

Despite controversy regarding the authorship and date of the *Vedanta Sutra,* the general view attributes the text to Sage Badarayana. It is called *Brahma Sutra* because 'it is an exposition of the doctrine of *Brahman*'; it is also known as *Sariraka Sutra* or the *Moksha Sutra.* In its collection of 555 verses based exclusively on logic, the *Sutra* is infused with abstrusely succinct philosophical statements of eternal relevance. These maxims are a necessary study for *sabdartha-vicara,* which is required to understand the *Upanishads.* Also known as the *Vedanta-Mimamsa,* the *Sutra* investigates the Vedantic thought that delves into the embodied soul, the *Atman.*

Categorised as a rare book, the *Sutra* rewards its interpreter or seeker, 'in accordance with his merits'. Sectioned into four chapters, it 'describes the philosophico-theological views of the *Upanishads*', beginning with *samanvaya* (reconciliation) that anchors on the centrality of *Brahman.* The first chapter deals with the nature of Reality, its relation to world—*jagat,* and individual—*jiva,* encompassing the Vedanta-*vakyas* leading to *ekvakyata*—oneness of thought. The second chapter (*avirodha*) of the commentary carries criticism from the opposing schools of thought and 'gives an account of the nature of the dependence of the world on God'; following this is the third chapter with methods (*sadhana*) for realising the *Atman-Brahman.*

Nothing stops. Nor is it intended any other way; a vital truth that the wise have reminded the living about. Indian spiritual heritage offers *the* most liberating knowledge about Death, and yet the practicality of its wisdom is severely lacking in the workings of the civilisational ethos. An undesirable fear surrounds the idea (about Death) that is baseless and entrenched in ignorance. The great litterateur, Harivansh Rai Bachchan, penned it rather eloquently, 'A body of clay, a mind full of play, a moment's life—that's me'.

During the month-long online symposium titled Global Festival of Oneness 2020, dedicated to Adi Shankara, Shakuntala Gawde, a scholar of Vedanta studies and Sanskrit, highlighted the Acharya's views on mortality as presented in his commentary on the *Brahma Sutra.* According to Gawde, Shankara begins by addressing *vairagya* and its role in achieving a purposeful end to life in chapters three and four, which deal with *sadhana* and *phalla*, respectively. The Vedantic scholar went on to provide other literary references, namely, the third chapter of Adi Shankara's *Brhadaranyaka bhasya*, wherein he explains, 'death in the form of organs and objects is bondage'. Delving into the individual's '*krama mukti*' (gradual salvation), the Acharya discusses in detail the embodied soul's (i) Departure, (ii) Transmigration, and the eventual (iii) Liberation.

According to the Great Master, the soul departs from the physical body accompanied by the *pancha maha bhutas* (the five primordial elements). Quoting the *Chandogya* Upanishad, in his commentary (III.1.1), Adi Shankara writes: 'In order to obtain another body, the soul goes enveloped (by subtle elements) (as appears from) the question and explanation.'

The Acharya's reasoning substantiates that in the absence of these limiting adjuncts, all souls would directly attain liberation, and the entirety of scriptures would be meaningless, since the *Sutra* is primarily a *Moksha Shastra* (Scripture for Liberation). The *Sutra* concludes with the fruits of *Brahmavidya.* It also describes at length the onward path of the *Atman*, 'along the two parts of the gods and the fathers and the nature of the release from which there is no return'.

Being the first commentary on the *Vedanta Sutra*, Adi Shankara's writing explains the concealed meaning of the aphorisms with an outline in the introduction. Herein, he explicates the 'root cause analysis' of *samsara* while clarifying that the following study is not intended as random reading; it is meant for those who are desirous of *Brahman jigyasa.* In the words of a contemporary wise man, '*jisse moksha ki iccha ho, wahi brahmajnana ko khojta hai!*'

Adi Shankara establishes in the commentary that the primary reason *samsara* exists is because of ignorance and its consequence (*adhyasa*), meaning the individual mistakes the Self for the non-self and conversely. He defines *adhyasa* 'as the appearance, in the form of remembrance, of one thing previously perceived, in another'; '*adhyaso nama atasmims tadbuddhih, smrtirupah paratra purvadrstavabhasah*' (Introduction, pp. 10–13).

Furthermore, the only reference to his defining the term *avidya* is also available in the introduction of the commentary: 'The learned men regard this superimposition thus defined as *avidya'—tam etam evamlaksanam adhyasam pandita avidyeti manyante* (Introduction, p. 19, line 2).

The premise of Adi Shankara's *Brahma Sutra Bhasya* is to stress that realisation of the Supreme is only through Upanishadic wisdom, logic, and experience. Vacaspati Misra, a renowned ninth-century philosopher of Advaita Vedanta, designated Shankara's commentary as '*prasanna gambhiram*'. It is acknowledged by many Vedantic scholars and theologians as his finest writing.

A closer scrutiny of Acharya Shankara's literature highlights another equally significant facet of his scholarship, his attention to language. In his commentary on the *Sutra* (I.iii.28), while discussing 'that creation comes out of the words', Acharya refutes the grammarians' sphota theory of words.

According to Woodroffe, in this theory, 'the impression created in the mind on hearing a sound (e.g. cow) expressive of meaning and itself expressed by the letters constituting the sound (e.g. cow).' However, Adi Shankara states, 'the letters of which a word consists, assisted by a certain order and number, have through traditional use entered into a connection with a definite sense. At the time when they are employed, they present themselves as such to the understanding, which, after having apprehended the several letters in succession, finally comprehends the entire aggregate, and they thus unerringly intimate to the understanding their definite sense' (Radhakrishnan).

Acharya's vocabulary across the spectrum of his writings echoes that 'the letters are the word'; hence, the exactness in his application of the same. Adi Shankara's scientific use of expressions and phrases exhibits a sense of discipline that resonates with his ascetic exterior and monism of being. As a commentator, a poet, and a teacher, the Advaitin regularly jolts the inquirer from stupor with his acerbic wit and occasionally, a hint of sarcasm. If you ask me, he was candid with a smile.

The special rank accorded to commentator Shankara is for unravelling the implicit and presenting it explicitly with remarkable dexterity. This is most evident in his commentaries on the following *Upanishads*: the *Chandogya*, the *Brhadaranyaka*, the *Taittiriya*, the *Aitareya*, the *Svetasvatara*, the *Kena*, the *Katha*, the *Isa*, the *Prasna*, the *Mundaka*, the *Mandukya*, the *Atharvasikha*, the *Atharvasiras*, and the *Nrsimhatapaniya*.

The first Upanishad that the Acharya wrote a commentary for was the *Taittiriya*, consisting of three chapters on the One-with-no-second

(*Brahman*). The scripture belongs to the (Krishna) *Yajur Veda*. The commentary probes into the *purusharthas* of *bhoga and apavarga* that exist within the intellect (2.1.1). 'The most profound definition of God' is ensconced in *Taittiriya* Upanishad in the statement: *satyam jnanam anantam brahma—Brahman* is Truth, Knowledge, Infinite. In the introduction, Shankara provides the core of his interpretation of the Upanishad by saying:

> The Self, as such, is Brahma:
> And from the knowledge of Brahman flows liberation
> Consisting in the eradication of ignorance.
> Hence is commenced this Upanisad, which is calculated
> to lead to the acquisition of the knowledge of Brahman.
>
> —*Adi Shankaracharya,*
> *Taittiriya-bhasya*

Bhasya on *Mandukya* Upanishad

Adi Shankara's commentary on the shortest and acknowledged as the most powerful Upanishad, the *Mandukya*, is a highly regarded Vedanta text. It is the concluding part of the *Atharva Veda*. '*Mandukyam ekam eva alam mumukshunam vimuktye*—for the liberation of the *mumukshū* or seeker, the *Māndūkya* alone is enough; and if you are able to understand the true meaning of this single Upanishad, there may not be a necessity to study any other Upanishad, not even the *Chhāndogya* or the *Brihadāranyaka*, because the theme of the *Māndūkya* Upanishad is a direct approach to the depths of human nature.'

Adi Shankara interprets each of the twelve statements called *mantras,* as well as Gaudapada's *Mandukya Karika* of four chapters, in this commentary. According to him, the scripture's knowledge is nestled in the *karika*; *so'yamātmā chatushpāt*, the fourfold stages of *jagrat*—awake, *svapna*—dream, *sushupti*—deep sleep, and *turiya*—spiritual transcendence. A mature understanding is crucial for the assimilation of *Mandukya's* subtle and direct teaching. The first seven *mantras* of the text are about the fourth stage (*turiya*) of the *Atman*, interestingly, without any mention of the term. It is Shankara's commentary and his dada guru, Gaudapada's *Mandukya Karika*, that refers to the term '*turiya-turiya*'.

The Upanishad commences with the *mantra* 'Om', which is imbued with *nada* and *bindu* (*chandra-bindu*). Woodroffe's treatise, *The Garland of Letters,* provides a heightened description of the *mantra*: 'This is both the efficient and material Cause of the universe, which is Its form or body. *Nada* is the *Mantra* name for the first going forth of Power which gathers itself together in massive strength (*Ghani-bhuta*) as *Bindu* to create the universe, and which *Bindu*, as so creating, differentiates into a Trinity of Energies which are symbolised by A, U, M. *Nada* and *Bindu* thus represent the unmanifested 'fourth' (*turiya*) state, immediately before the manifestation of the world, in which animate life exists in the three conditions of dreamless sleep, dream, and waking.' This encapsulates the philosophical import of Advaita Vedanta.

The *Mandukya* emphasises that all *nama-rupa* (names and forms) of objects in the world arise from 'Om'. Speaking on the *Mantras* 8 to 12 of the *Mandukya,* the Great Master enlightens on the three-fold hierarchy of 'Om' *vicara*, which is, in actuality, *atma-vicara.* He begins with *Om* as the *Pratika* (symbol) of divine reality, followed by an explanation of the entirety of sound manifested in the composition of the *Mantra*, A U M, before coalescing into *maunam* (Quietude) wherein 'Om' is *Brahman.* Thus, the seeker becomes aware of the non-dual knowledge of the *Mantra*; that contemplation on the *Pratika* leads to the realisation of the Self as 'one vital Sakti'.

In order to grasp the subtlety of the actual meaning of quietude—*maunah* in the *Mantra* 'Om', Acharya's definition of the *mantra* in another ancient text, called *Sanatsujatiya*, which he is said to have authored, is particularly relevant. Signifying contemplation and quoting the scriptures, Adi Shanakra says, '*Brahman* is "*maunam*" because neither the *Vedas* nor the mind can reach (describe) Him. He is the source from which the *Vedas* have arisen. Or, He is the consciousness because of which the words of the *Vedas* are pronounced. He shines as effulgence itself. The *Taittiriya* Upanishad says, "That from which the words return along with the mind without reaching it is *Brahman.*"' Adi Shankara elaborates on 'the conception of state through A U M' in *Pancikaranam*, the smallest booklet written by him, and one that carries only five verses.

> Now, 'A', the waking personality, should be resolved into 'U', the dream personality, and the 'U' into 'M', that is, the deep-sleep personality. Again the 'M' should be reduced into '*Aum*'and the '*Aum*' into 'I'. I am, the Atman, the Witness of all, the absolute, of the nature of Pure Consciousness; I am neither nescience nor even its effect, but I am Brahman alone, Eternally Pure, Ever Enlightened, Eternally Free, and Existence Absolute. I am the Bliss Absolute, One without a second and the Innermost Consciousness.
>
> —*Adi Shankaracharya,*
> *Pancikaranam (2)*

Given that a study of the Self is the subject of the *Mandukya*, it proceeds by employing the methodology of analysis and synthesis to illustrate the same. The explanation rendered through object and subject focuses on the investigation of the Subject—*Brahman*. Beginning with the awake—*jagrat* stage, wherein, through the *upadhi,* the embodied soul experiences the world. The scripture calls this first condition '*Bahishprajnaah*—It is conscious only of what is outside, not conscious of what is inside.'

The *jivatman* or the Upanishadic *visva* is defined as '*saptānga ekonavimśatimukhah*: seven-limbed and nineteen-mouthed is this consciousness', which makes the individual aware of the outside world. In its *prathama-pada* (first quarter), the scripture addresses the consciousness in this state as *Vaisvanara,* thereby establishing precedence because the knowledge of succeeding *padas* is contingent on his *jnana.*

Establishing the continuum of the Veda-Vedanta, the antiquity of the Vedantic teaching can be traced to the Rig-Vedic hymn, Purusha-Sukta, which begins 'by saying that all the heads, all the eyes, and all the feet that we see in this world are the heads, eyes, and feet of the Virat-Purusha, or the Cosmic Being'. In its instruction, the third *mantra* of *Mandukya* and Gaudapada's *Karika* sums up the experience of the insentient in the awake state by addressing God as *Virat.* Encompassing the microcosm and macrocosm is the grand vision experienced by Arjun when the Supreme Being reveals by saying:

pasya me partha rupani
sataso 'tha sahasrasah
nanavidhani divyani
nanavarnakrtini ca

Behold, O Partha (Arjuna),
My forms, a hundred-fold, a thousand-fold,
various in kind, divine,
of various colours and shapes.

—*Bhagavadgita, 11.5*

In the subsequent dream (*svapna*) state, the awareness is directed inward into the arterial network of the mind. The *Mandukya* calls it *antah-prajna*, heightened with 'subtle perception' and wherein *Atman* is recognised as *taijasa.* The fourth *mantra* of the scripture declares: '*svapna-sthāno'ntah-prajñah saptānga ekonavimśati- mukhah pravivikta-bhuk taijaso dvītiyah pādah*'. In this condition, Gaudapada's *Karika* calls God *Hiranyagarbha.* Moving from the gross to the subtle, the relation between hiranyagarba and taijasa in *svapna* is the same as that of *Vaisvanara* and *visvain jagrat.*

From the point of view of the individual, the deep sleep state is difficult to comprehend, 'but it is simple from the point of view of Cosmic Experience'.

The concentricity of *Mandukya*'s instruction deepens in the fifth *mantra,* which enlightens about the deep sleep condition called *sushupti*; the merged condition of the waking and dream states. Herein, the complete cessation of activity of the individual's mind renders it unconscious. Experiencing *ekibhutah*—'this is complete absorption of the mind into itself'. The scripture calls this third aspect *Prajnana-ghanah*, 'undifferentiated mass of consciousness'. The embodied soul, earlier as *visva* then *taijasa*, is ultimately *prajna*; 'the consciousness which is in its own pristine nature, knowing everything and not being associated with anything external'.

Sushupti cannot be mistaken as the 'absence of experience, but it is the experience of absence', 'of uniform blankness'. The scripture's methodology of differentiation as object and subject dissolves at this stage. *Virat* is the God during *jagrat*, and in the state of *svapna*, he is called *Hiranyagarbha.* In deep sleep, the corresponding God is known as *Isvara.* Given the stage-wise analysis, it is no surprise that the individual in *sushupti* experiences *ananda*—bliss of the *Satcitananda.*

Thereafter, continuing its explanation of deep sleep, the *Mandukya's* sixth *mantra* discusses *Maya* that works through *Isvara* for the creation of *jagat*—the world. The scripture points towards the Vedic proclamation, '*Ekam sat vipra bahudha vadanti*, the One existence is regarded as many by the great sages. They behold the One as many. Many names are given to the One.'

In actuality, by analysing the three states, the Upanishad is in fact directing the inquirer towards the fourth state of *turiya* for discovering his true nature—*Brahman.* Therefore, the seventh *mantra* of the *Mandukya* Upanishad is acknowledged by the wise as 'the most powerful *mantra* in the entire Vedantic literature' as it reveals the grand truth. Proclaimed as the 'highest expression of Vedanta', Advaitin Shankara's interpretation of the seventh *mantra* of the Upanishad is Advaita in a nutshell.

Adi Shankara's commentary enlightens the seeker about the seventh *mantra* by the use of the words *Neti Neti* (not this, not this). Dwelling on the profundity of the scripture's inherent *Mahavakya*—'I am *Brahman*', Acharya poses questions that an ordinary mind asks; evident in the template of objections and answers seen in his commentaries. In the Upanishad, verse 7 provides one of *the* most profound and accurate descriptions of *Brahman* in the entire spectrum of Vedantic wisdom.

> *nāntaḥprajñaṃ na bahiḥprajñaṃ nobhayataḥprajñaṃ na prajñānaghanaṃ na prajñaṃ nāprajñam |*
> *adṛśyam avyavahāryam agrāhyam alakṣaṇam acintyam avyapadeśyam ekātma-pratyaya-sāraṃ prapañcopaśamaṃ śāntaṃw śivam advaitaṃ caturthaṃ manyante sa ātmā sa vijñeyaḥ*
> || 7 ||

> *Turīya* is not that which is conscious of the internal (subjective) world, nor that which is conscious of the external (objective) world, nor that which is conscious of both, nor that which is a mass all sentiency, nor that which is simple consciousness, nor that which is insentient. (It is) unseen (by any sense organ), not related to anything, incomprehensible (by the mind), uninferable, unthinkable, indescribable, essentially of the nature of Consciousness constituting the Self alone, negation of all phenomena, the Peaceful, all Bliss and the Non-dual. This is what is known as the fourth (*Turīya*). This is the Ātman, and it has to be realised.

The commentary clarifies that neither the waker, nor the dreamer, the deep sleeper, nor the unmentioned fourth, *turiya*, is the subject and not an object of senses that can be experienced through sight, taste, touch, hearing, breathing, nor is it an organ of an individual's experience of mobility. Acharya's direct instruction states that such a condition cannot be inferred. In Gaudapada's *Karika*, the second chapter on 'the falsity of the world' is devoted to the fine understanding of one word through reason and logic. Verse 32 presents a 'stunning' premise illuminating the doctrine of non-origination (*ajata-vada*):

> There is no dissolution, no origination, none in bongage,
> None striving or aspiring for salvation, and none liberated.
> This is the highest truth.

With a host of examples, the Great Master establishes that without ground there cannot be falsity, error-free cannot exist without error; thus, *turiya*—the *Atman* is not a void or an experience of nothingness. It *is* the Self (*Brahman*), the underlying awareness, the existence of *jagrat*, *svapna*, and *sushupti*. Pure consciousness has the appearance or superimposition of the three states, but it remains all through the *Atman-Brahman* Self. Therefore, Shankara argues that in the absence of 'snake in the rope' or 'silver in nacre' or 'pot in clay', and so on, there cannot be any relation between real and unreal. He asserts that in such a context, there is no use of language; only knowledge of 'intuitive experience' can allow one to realise the non-duality of it all.

In response to the probable questions emerging from *Mandukya's* seventh *mantra*, such as what is the practical use of Advaita? Adi Shankara avers, 'the total cessation of sorrow and *paramananda prapti*—attainment of eternal bliss and peace'. Is the resultant of spiritual seeking nothing—*shuniya*? Not so, states the Great Master. Is there a purpose in knowing about the *turiya-Atman*? The Advaitin affirms that *turiya* is not a state of *Atman* but *Atman,* hence, removes the 'hunger for *anatman*'; a concept borrowed from the Buddhist doctrine of 'no-self'.

The realisation of 'I am *Brahman*' transcends the boundaries of fear, temptation, and limitation. This is *moksha prapti*—enlightenment, the ultimate liberation. The explanation highlights Advaita as the instantly available wisdom—'right here, right now', through knowledge of the Self, embodied as *Satcitananda.* Acharya's *Mandukya* commentary conveys to the inquirer to exist as awareness, in which the mind-body framework appears, instead of living with the erroneous perception of the mind-body framework wherein awareness appears!

Adi Shankara's commentary on the Upanishad enlightens us about the fundamental cause of erroneous living, wherein the mind-body construct is not aware of the ground for error. Referring to the example of the rope-snake, Acharya explains that if the rope were not mistaken for a snake, there would be no *avidya* or *ajnanta.* More importantly, he stresses that reactions are the source of suffering, which is the reason for being aware of the existence of the rope but not its nature. Thereby deducing that Advaita Vedanta is a way of life that provides serenity and stamina simultaneously.

Bhasya on *Brhadaranyaka* Upanishad

Consisting of six chapters that are attached to the *Yajur Veda*, the Scripture (*Brhadaranyaka* Upanishad*)* is called '*Aranyaka*' since its place of instruction was a forest (*Aranya*) and because of its large (*Brhad*) size, it is known as *Brhadaranyaka*. This Upanishad reveals that 'knowledge (*sruti*) came with Creation, which means this knowledge remains as the non-dual consciousness'. According to Adi Shankara, the Upanishad is 'composed for the sake of those who wish to liberate themselves from the world, in order that they may acquire the knowledge that the Absolute *Brahman* and the individual are the same'.

In the introduction of Acharya Shankara's *Bhasya*, the purpose behind the writing is clearly stated when he says, 'Hence for the removal of the ignorance of man who is disgusted with this universe, this Upanishad is being commenced in order to inculcate the knowledge of *Brahman*, which is the very opposite of that ignorance.'

It is interesting that while examining Adi Shankara's *sahitya,* a curious analogy of a duster, chalk, and blackboard springs to mind in the context of Advaita and *avidya*—ignorance. As if with each text, the Advaitin wiped clean the blackboard of the seeker's mind (of its previous content) and wrote afresh about *jnana*, reiterating that wisdom can only be sought by removal of ignorance.

The introduction of the *Brhadaranyaka* commentary also establishes the connect—*sambandh*—between the scripture and the ceremonial sections of the *Veda*. Quoting the Upanishad (6.5.1–6.5.4), Adi Shankara says, 'That *Brahman* (the *Vedas*) has come down the line of Prajapati and variously branched off among us. It is without beginning and end—self-born or eternal. Salutations to that *Brahman* (the *Vedas*) and salutations to the teachers who have followed it.'

The wisdom of the Scripture (*Brhadaranyaka* Upanishad) is ensconced in its three *kanda-s*, namely, *Madhu kanda*, *Yajnavalkya kanda*, or *Muni kanda*, and *Khila kanda*. The structure of the text systematically guides the aspirant through a corridor of philosophical instructions beginning with an *upadesa* on Advaita Vedanta in *Madhu kanda*, followed by establishing the legitimacy of the *upadesa* with articulated reasoning in *Muni kanda*, before concluding with the offering of *upasana-s* or modes of meditation in

Khila kanda. According to Shankara, the Upanishad actually begins from the third chapter of *Madhu kanda.*

Acharya's construct of *sambandh* (relation between subject and object) rests on four themes. It acknowledges the entirety of the Vedic canon, thereby validating an integrated presence of *jnana kanda* and *karma kanda* in Advaita Vedanta. This can be interpreted to an extent as Shankara's endorsement of *Maya*—the power of *Brahman*, being instrumental in Self-realisation; giving credence to duality, leading the way for non-duality. In order to illustrate the point, a reference to *Sadana Panchakam* is required here.

Popularly perceived as Acharya Shankara's final utterances, *Sadana Panchakam,* also known as *Sadana Sopana*, is a compilation of five verses that is said to have been composed by him, especially at the behest of his disciples, shortly before taking the *mahasamadhi* at Kedarnath. The first verse of the text states clearly Acharya's devotion to the *Vedas*:

> ***vedo-nityam-adhiyatam***—Let the scriptures be studied daily
> ***taduditam karmasvanushthiyatam***—Let those Karmas enjoined in the scriptures be well performed
> ***tenesasya vidhiyatam apachitih***—Through the practice of Karma, let God be worshipped
> ***kamye matistyajyatam***—Let the mind be taken away from desire-engendered actions
> ***papaughah paridhuyatam***—Let all sins be destroyed
> ***bhavasukhe dosho'nusandhiyatam***—Let the aspirant enquire into the defects and imperfections of the pleasures of this transmigratory life.
>
> —*Adi Shankaracharya,*
> *Sadhna Panchkam, verse 1*

Secondly, Acharya Shankara's construct about the *sambandh* reiterates that *atma-jnana* is possible only through *sruti-jnana*—the knowledge of scriptures. He emphasises that liberation (*moksha prapti)* is attainable through the singularity of Advaita and not the ritualistic traditions. Quoting the scripture, Shankara says, 'It is well known in the world that rites are the means to attain all our life's ends; and their performance depends on wealth, which cannot possibly confer immortality. This can be attained only through Self-knowledge independently of rites.' (2.5.15)

In Advaita Vedanta, for any form of knowledge to be a *pramana*, it needs to qualify three crucial parameters: (i) It is a statement in the absence of any contradiction; (ii) It is of a unique (*anadikta*) nature; and (iii) It is of useful purpose. The *Vedas*, Acharya asserts, satisfy all three prerequisites; hence, they are integral to *sabda pramana.*

In the final analysis regarding *sambandh*, to the spiritual aspirant, Adi Shankara imparts that *karma kanda* is relevant to *moksha prapti*, because it initiates *citasuddhi* (purification of the mind), which prepares the spiritual candidate (*adhikari*) for *jnana kanda*. The Great Master writes that the source or means (*pramana*) of knowledge is perception (*pratyaksha*), inference (*anumana*), and 'scriptural testimony' (*sabda*).

According to some scholars, the first chapter of the Upanishad is known as ghata *bhasya* because of the analogy used (of pot and clay) to illustrate cause (*karana*) and effect (*karya*); while there are those who state the frequency of the word '*ghata*' as the prime reason for the title. Acharya's commentary explains that cause and effect enjoy a constant existence; the presence of clay is evidence of the potential pot (*ghata*) even though it is not there in plain sight. Hence, the non-manifested effect exists (potentially) in the existence of the cause. This is called *Siddhanta.* To the opposing *Samkhyas* (Buddhist sect), Adi Shankara clarifies that form or appearance or manifestation is not the cause.

Similarly, debating with the logicians about *karana-karya* (cause-action) with reference to obstruction (*avarana*), Acharya articulates with the analogy of a pot and a potter. The figurative use of language by Shankara is indicative of his subtlety of thought while deliberating on Advaita; for instance, his preference for the words manifest and non-manifestation instead of creation and destruction.

Viewed by some scholars as 'designed to answer academic criticism', Adi Shankara's commentary on the *Brhadaranyaka* Upanishad is essentially a comprehensive verse-by-verse explanation of the scripture. His pragmatism in realising the need to save the *Upanishads* and Advaita in the hostile environment of his time led him to undertake the task of scripting voluminously, thus enhancing the circumference of the then-existing literature on Advaita Vedanta. Undeniably, the *Brhadaranyaka* Upanishad is an intricate 'Forest of wisdom' that has two distinct routes offering separate reachable destinations, and the compass for safe passage lies in Adi Shankara's commentary—*bhasya*.

Recognised as 'the greatest of his commentaries on the *Upanishads*', it is in the commentary on the *Brhadaranyaka* Upanishad that Adi Shankara decisively explicates the *Brahman-Atman vicara* (*Brahmavidya*) as being the central purport of Vedanta *jnana* in general and of this scripture, in particular.

In addition, the remarkable display of his 'powerful dialects' that defeats the views of the *Mimamaskas*, *Vaisesikas*, *Naiyayikas*, and supporters of the *bhedabheda* (difference-cum-identity), is another important reason for Adi Shankara's commentary to be hailed as truly exceptional. The essence of the Upanishad's teaching is that everything has an external character, an internal nature, and a transcendent reality, and none can be ignored while evaluating anything and everything. As the first verse of *khila kanda* declares—'*That is the whole*; the *whole* is *this*: from the *whole* rises up the *whole*; and having seized the *whole* of the *whole*, the *whole* alone remains.'

Adi Shankara's *bhasya* on the Upanishad illuminates that knowledge necessitates an entirety of vision, not an incomplete, 'partial look'. More importantly, knowledge is not information, nor is it a task undertaken by *buddhi*—intellect, but it is *anubhava*—experience. Hence, *jnana* and *anubhava* are two sides of the same coin (for the individual—*jiva*). Wisdom—*jnana* is Being. It would be reasonable to state that Acharya's thorough examination of *sruti jnana*, combined with his seasoned rationale, raised the calibre of scholarship exponentially for commentators and scholars in the future.

srutyacaryaprasadena drdho bodho yada bhavet,
nirastasesasamsaranidanah purusastada.

Through the grace of a spiritual teacher, when
a seeker gains a clear and direct experience of
the supreme Self as expounded in the scriptures,
he, the Realised, Becomes free from all ignorance,
which is the foundation for the entire experience
of this world of plurality.

—*Adi Shankaracharya,*
Vakya Vrtti, 50.

Bhasya on *Bhagavadgita*

An integral constituent of the *prasthana-traya*, The *Bhagavadgita* is addressed by Adi Shankara as the '*Sarva Vedanta Shastra Sangrah*' (Br.Up. 2.4/4.5). The introduction to his '*Gita-shastra*' outlines an apparently religious, however, an intrinsically spiritual framework for the seeker. His commentary is recognised as 'the most ancient of the existing ones'. The Acharya states in the introduction that 'the aim of the *Gita* is the complete suppression of the world of becoming in which all action occurs'—'*gitasastrasya prayojanam param nihsreyasam, sahetukasaya samsarasya atyantoparamalaksanam*'.

Describing the structure of the commentary, Acharya Shankara explains: 'In this *Gita*, there are three distinct parts, each part consisting of six chapters. These three parts deal with the three words of the great Upanisadic saying, '*Tattvamasi*, thou art That', with a view to finding out their real meanings. The first six chapters are concerned with the word *tvam* (thou); the following six chapters determine the meaning of the word *tat* (that); and the last six reveal the essential identity of *tvam* and *tat*.

Expounding on the scripture's fundamental teaching, of the 'two-fold Vedic Religion of Works and Renunciation that maintains order in the universe', Adi Shankara uses the term *Dvividha-nishtha* (two-fold Vedic religion) in the introduction to discuss the nature of Dharma; *Pravrtti-dharma* (Religion of Works) and *Nivrtti-dharma* (Religion of Renunciation). The word *dharma* in *Gita-Bhasya* carries a more refined interpretation than its theological meaning. It signifies lifestyle, reflective of *karma yoga* and *pravrtti-dharma,* the Great Master says, for the purpose of *abhyudaya*, the Vedic term for *dharma, artha, kama*, while *nivrtti-dharma*, as an indicator of *jnana yoga*, is meant to achieve *nihsreyasa*, the Vedic term for salvation.

The manner in which these lifestyles are presented, according to Advaitin Shankara, the *Gita* 'treats a specific subject with a specific object and bears a specific relation (to the subject and object). A knowledge of its teaching leads to the realisation of all human aspirations'. Interestingly, the Acharya's eloquent presentation of *pravrtti* and *nvrtti dharma-s* in the introduction of the commentary remains exclusive and unique. According to scholars, none of the other commentaries by him has the same luminosity of idea as that of the *Gita-Bhasya*.

Making the idea timeless, Adi Shankara connects *pravrtti-dharma* and *nivrtti-dharma* with the hierarchy of the *varna-ashram*; 'For it was by the preservation of spiritual life that the Vedic Religion could be preserved, since thereon depend all distinctions of caste and religious order.' It is in the context of the divine incarnation of Visnu as Krishna in the *Mahabharata* that Acharya Shankara makes this observation. In Advaita Vedanta, it is *nivrtti-dharma* that is posited, while *pravrtti-dharma* is negated on account of its nature. It is the Great Master's *Gita-Bhasya* that brings forth the idea that both lifestyles contribute towards sustaining the world. *Kama* is the *karana* for the individual—*jiva*—to go astray. It is a 'degeneration of righteousness', comments the *Bhasyakar* Shankara.

From an instructional perspective, the Great Master enlightens on the origins of the teaching traditions of both the *dharmas*: 'He first created the *Prajapatis* (Lords of creatures) such as *Marichi* and caused them to adopt the *pravrtti-dharma*, the Religion of Works. He then created others, such as *Sanaka* and *Sanandana*, and caused them to adopt the *nivrtti-dharma*, the Religion of Renunciation, characterised by knowledge and indifference to worldly objects.'

For the householder, of the path of action that aims at prosperity, Adi Shankara says *pravrtti-dharma*, when performed with the attitude of offering to the Gods (*Isvara arpana buddhi*), with renunciation of fruits, this lifestyle enables purification of the mind (*citasuddhi*) necessary for liberation. Thus, the Acharya ranks the Religion of Works prior to the Religion of Renunciation. In terms of his Advaita *vicara*, this is a gigantic leap that qualifies the seeker with a chance to become eligible for *moksha* through karma yoga.

Interpreting the *Gita's* chapter two, verse 53, Adi Shankara speaks of the restlessness or distraction of the mind (*canchalta*) that *nivrtti-dharma* cannot possess and the need for '*nishtha*'—resoluteness by the seeker. Herein is the understated voice of the Advaitin Shankara, suggesting wellness to the individual by developing a meditative disposition while performing his responsibilities (of *pravrtti-dharma*) in the field of *karma-yoga*.

srutivipratipanna te
yada sthasyati niscala
samadhav acala buddhis
tada yogam avapsyasi

When thy intelligence, which is bewildered by the Vedic texts,
Shall stand unshaken and stable in spirit (Samadhi),
Then shalt thou attain to insight (yoga)

—*Bhagavadgita, II.,53*

Based on disposition (*svabhava*), an inquirer/seeker can be of three kinds: *karmatha*, *karamyogi*, and *sanyasin*. According to the *Mahabharat Gita*, those who are *karmatha* are called 'yogis' and the ones who are *sanyasin* are called *samkhya*. In the *Gita*, the term *samkhya* does not refer to the school of thought by that name; nor does *yoga* connote Patanjali *yoga*. 'To know the Good, you need to be Good' (Plato) is the core import of the *Gita's* teachings. It seeks from the individual 'to choose the good and realise it by conscious effort'. Emphasising the individual's freedom of choice and the manner in which he exercises, the teacher of the *Bhagavadgita* directs by saying:

esa te 'bhihita samkhye
buddhir yoge tu imam srnu
buddhya yukto yaya partha
karmabandham prahasyasi

This wisdom (buddhi) has been imparted to you
from the standpoint of Self-realisation (Sankhya).
But listen to this (wisdom) from the standpoint of
(Karma) Yoga.

—*Bhagavadgita, II.,39*

A vital aspect while studying Adi Shankara's *sahitya* is to discern the fine print regarding the workings of Advaita Vedanta. Particularly in the context of commentaries, as an Advaitin, his writing exhibits the discipline of instruction; first of his kind, a dialectician and analyst of classical thought who reduces the loftiness of the scriptures and widens their reach by facilitating comprehension. With the '*Gita-Sastra*' as well, the Acharya's sterling contribution is the manner in which he has extracted the underlying meaning of the scripture.

For instance, the discourse on Food in the *Gita* in chapter 17, verse 7, speaks of the philosophy that dictates, 'We are what we eat'.

aharas tv apisarvasya
trividho bhavati priyah
yajnas tapas tatha danam
tesam bhedam imam srnu

Even the food which is dear to all is of three kinds.
So are the sacrifices, austerities, and gifts.
Hear thou the distinction of these.

In the *Gita* commentary, Shankara candidly states: 'what sort of food—which is divided into three classes, viz., that which is savoury and oleaginous, and so on—is dear to the *Sattvic*, *Rajasic*, and *Tamasic* men respectively, so that a man may know that he is one of *Sattva* or of *Rajas* or of *Tamas* as indicated by his own partiality for one or another particular class of food—such as the savoury and the oleaginous—and then give up the *Rajasic* and *Tamasic* food and resort to Sattvic one. Similarly, the object of the threefold division here made of sacrifice and the like according to the *Sattva* and other *gunas* is to show how a man may find out and give up the *Rajasic* and *Tamasic* ones and resort exclusively to the *Sattvic* ones'.

Distilling the undisclosed context of well-being, the Great Master talks about the different types of food—*ahar*—and its impact as mentioned in the verses 8 to 10, chapter 17, of the *Gita*: 'The foods which increase life, energy, strength, health, joy, and cheerfulness, which are savoury and oleaginous, substantial and agreeable, are dear to the *Sattvic*; the foods that are bitter, sour, saline, excessively hot, pungent, dry, and burning, are liked by the *Rajasic*, causing pain, grief, and disease; the food which is stale, tasteless, putrid and rotten, refuse and impure, is dear to the *Tamasic*.' It is the cogent expression while discussing the philosophy of food and its subsequent manifestation in the individual's personality that renders Adi Shankara's narration in his writings, particularly in the commentaries, exemplary.

Intended for maximum readership, the Great Master's commentaries on the *Prasthana-traya* are iconic testimonials of his intellectual prowess. Aside from the quintessential Advaita method of *apavada*, these display explicit employment of an 'umbrella' concept of *adhyaropa*—negation of a superimposition. By devoting the entire introduction of the commentary on the *Brahma Sutra* to *adhyasa* (superimposition), Acharya Shankara establishes clarity beyond a doubt on the matter.

Even though most texts on Advaita Vedanta mention *avidya*, an overwhelming presence of the term is absent from the Great Master's commentaries. Wherever mentioned, he defines the term by a threefold differentiation. More importantly, as an Advaitin, his endeavours resonate with the Vedanta's solution-centric approach and not problem-harping.

Though implied in the *sruti*, the idea of *jivanmukti* emerges with precision in Adi Shankara's commentaries. Similarly, regarding the scriptural meditational techniques of *vastu* and *purusa* tantram, it is his writing of the *bhasya-s* that highlight the potency of these vital practices. In addition, the *gyana karma upasana vyavastha,* a system that encapsulates the entire Vedic knowledge in a single equation, is another landmark contribution by the illustrious Advaitin.

The use of the term, *dvividha-nishtha*, reiterates Shankara's departure from convention with regard to language. On the Advaita Vedanta circuit of scholarship, *dvividha-nishtha* does not find frequent mention. More importantly, regarding *maya* (the creative power of *Brahman*), it is interesting to observe that Adi Shankara's commentaries do not dwell excessively on the idea because he establishes a causal relationship between *maya* and *avidya*; his views on ignorance are as afore mentioned.

Viewed as a religious text, most approach the *Bhagavadgita* seeking answers to dilemmas arising from mundane irrationalities. However, the Great Master's grasp of the Scripture is spiritual; hence, his commentary on the *Gita* delves into the subtleties of the meanings of the verses. For instance, clarifying on the ever-contested concern of attaining salvation by *karma* or *jnana*, in his commentary on *Sanatsujatiya*, the Acharya says: 'Liberation is accomplished by wisdom, but wisdom does not spring without the purification of the heart. Therefore, for the purification of the heart, one should perform all acts of speech, mind, and body, prescribed in the *srutis* and *smritis*, dedicating them to the Supreme Lord.'

jnanenaiva moksah siddhyati kimtu tad eva jnanam
sattvasuddhim vind notpadyate... tasmat sattvasuddhyartham
sarvesvaram uddisya sarvani vanmanahkayalaksanani
srautasmartani karmani samacaret

The underlying idea of *bhakti* is cardinal to the *Gita* because devotion steers wisdom—*jnana*. Given that the scripture is 'a mandate for action', it clarifies what an individual ought to do not only as a social being but also as a spiritual aspirant. Thus, Shankara's commentary reinforces by saying, '*karma-yoga* accompanied with the abandonment of the fruits of action is a means to Bliss'.

Interpreting verses 13 and 14 in chapter 12 of the *Gita*, the Great Master defines 'the true devotee' as: 'He hates nothing, not even that which causes him pain. He regards all beings as himself. He is friendly and compassionate. He is full of compassion for the distressed, i.e., he has offered security of life to all beings, he is a *samnyasin*. He does not regard anything as "mine" and is free from egoism, from the notion of "I". Pain and pleasure do not cause hatred and attachment. He remains unaffected when abused or beaten. He is always content; he thinks he has enough, whether he obtains or not the means of bodily sustenance. He is also satisfied whether he comes by a good thing or not. He is a Yogi, always steadfast in thought. He has a firm conviction regarding the essential nature of the Self. This *samnyasin* has directed to me exclusively his *manas*—purposes and thoughts—as well as his *Buddhi*—the faculty of determining. Such a devotee is dear to me.' The same truth is indicated in vii. 17—'I am very dear to the wise man and he is dear to me'—is here described at length.

Recognising that as a Scripture, the *Gita* consolidates *brahmavidya* and *yogashastra,* Shankara's commentary indicates the fundamental categories of existence: *ksara*, *aksara*, and *purusottama*. 'In samsara, there are two categories, we see, arranged in two separate groups of beings, spoken of as "purushas". One group consists of the perishable (*kshara*), and the other is the imperishable (*akshara*)—the contrary of the first.'

> There are these two beings in the world,
> The perishable and the imperishable:
> The perishable comprises all creatures;
> The immutable is called the imperishable
>
> —*Adi Shankaracharya,*
> *Gita-Sastra, 15:16*

The *Prakarana-s*

Enlightened as he was, Adi Shankara realised that the study of the Self as illumined in the scriptures necessitated an absolute understanding of the Vedantic terminology and concepts. Hence, he wrote the *Prakriya Grantha-s*, also called *Prakarana*—a series of handbooks/guides/manuals decoding the tenets of his doctrine of Advaita. These lucidly scripted instructional texts are in three volumes, compiled from the printed and available source material.

The remarkable attribute of the *Prakarana* is the brevity of meaning ensconced with Shankara's Advaita in no more than *eka sloka*—single verse; the Sanskrit of *eka sloka-s* is simple to assimilate, yet eloquent in the metaphysics of their import. The question and answer composition of these verses, in particular, is significantly appealing to the young and curious.

More importantly, the methodology of these writings is indicative of Adi Shankar's vision in extending tremendous leverage to the seeker in terms of the availability of time and place for comprehending the wisdom of the Veda-Vedanta. By this intention, his *Sahitya* becomes accessible to an assorted audience that includes the ordinary people, the scholarly, and the spiritually evolved.

Some of the prominent titles in the genre include *Vivekacudamani*, *Aparokshanubhuti*, *Atma-bodha*, *Upadesa Sahasri*, *Vakiya Vrtti*, *Pancikaranam*, and *Tattva-bodha*. It is worthwhile to mention here that from more than forty such texts, ascertaining the authenticity of authorship to even half remains an unfulfilled endeavour by many accomplished scholars of Vedanta and Advaitins themselves.

Reinforcing the criteria for initiating the process of inquiry on non-duality, through the *Prakarana*, Adi Shankara asks the candidate, firstly, to disassociate with finitude, thereby meaning that the seeker disengages his identity from any object that is a limited source of knowledge. Secondly, the seeker knows himself as pure Subject, the *saksin*—witness of all objects. Lastly, the seeker knows himself in the infinite quotient: '*Aham Brahmasmi*'.

Advaita Vedanta calls this the *jnana-yoga* or Path of Knowledge. With these guidelines, Acharya Shankara reminds us about the ever-present Reality (*Sat*): The individual *is* pure Consciousness; we *are* one with God. The irony, however, is that we are not aware of the *Sat*. Hence, the purpose of spiritual seeking is to remove the 'mistaken identity' of the body-mind construct; to rid oneself of the error (the thinking and feeling) that one is not free from.

The primary reason for our ignorance is a reminder of the Talmudic expression, 'We do not see things as they are. We see them as we are.' Adi Shankara's idea of non-duality provides the sight required to correct the error. Echoing the same thought, Advaitin Ramana Maharishi says, 'What greater fool is there than the one who does not seek his own good?'

> Rejoice eternally!!
> The heart rejoices at the feet of the Lord, who is the Self,
> shining within as 'I-I' eternally,
> so that there is no alternation of night and day.
> This will result in removal of ignorance of the Self.
>
> —*Ramana Maharishi,*
> *Crest Jewel of Discrimination*
> *('Vivekachudamani')*

Aparokshanubhuti

It is an established fact that 'where attention goes, energy flows', which is why Adi Shankara's instruction on Advaita emphatically seeks an exploration of *who am I*. His writing in the *Prakarana-s* resonates with the compendium of the Vedanta wisdom: Definition of Consciousness is 'Not this experience'; what is God? '*Saguna Brahman*'; Does the mind organ reveal *Brahman*? '*Brahman* transcends the reflected consciousness called *cidabhasa*', and so on.

One of the most recommended handbooks on Advaita Vedanta by Shankara is the text called *Aparokshanubhuti*. It deals with philosophical complexity and uses relatable similes to extrapolate. To the uninformed, the pithy appearance of the text can be misleading, as perhaps is the etymology of its title. The extracted meaning of *Aparokshanubhuti* is 'Direct realisation of the Absolute'. The characteristic of this work is that by the end of an earnest read, an experiential awakening takes place through one's own thinking, and the Self is realised.

The text is a compilation of 144 verses written succinctly. The non-dual teaching synthesises a multitude of disciplines, that is, literature, chemistry, sociology, mathematics, history, and others. It is the *prakarana* of *Aparokshanubhuti* that proclaims, 'Vedanta is not faith but a fact of life'. The guide begins with an invocation, in verses 1 and 2, followed by details about the four-fold qualification—*sadhana catuṣtha* from verse 3 to 10, primarily dwelling on the 'entry condition' for an inquirer/seeker.

Unless *vivek*, *vairagya*, *shat sampati* of *sama*, *dama*, *uparati*, *samadhan*, *tittiksha*, *shraddha*, and *mumukshutvam* are not absorbed by the candidate, even the slightest of progress towards Self-realisation is not possible. Consequently, ignorance will continue to determine the action—*karma,* and the individual will succumb to the confusion of cause (*karana*) and effect (*karya*).

Highlighting the relevance of the *sadhana catustha*, Adi Shankara says in verse 10, 'Only that person who is in possession of the said qualification (as means to knowledge) should reflect with a view to attaining Knowledge—*jnana*, desiring his own good'. Herein lies the understated learning of defining the four essentials intended for an individual's well-being, making it evident that our wellness is not a procurable state. It needs to be worked upon constantly and ought not to be taken for granted.

Taking the illustration of pot and clay, in the context of *karana-karya*, the succinct text discusses the falsity of name, form, and use, thereby stating that the object, pot, is the effect of the subject, clay. The former is merely an appearance or an unreal or a manifestation, and is false. The cause and subject that is the clay alone is real and true.

However, sharpening his argument with reason and logic, Acharya Shankara asserts that in the absence of substantiality of the subject, the clay as a pot, there is no *karana*. Hence, there is no real cause and effect. The deduction is arrived at by inquiry, that is, the application of *jnana* as exemplified in verses 11 to 15. Especially, the existential queries addressed in verse 12 indicate Shankara's concern for human despondency: '*Who am I? How is this (world) created? Who is its creator? Of what material is this (world) made? This is the way of that Vicara (enquiry).*'

Aparokshanubhuti scrutinises the realms of *Jiva*, *Jagat*, and *Isvara* in the light of name, form, and use. The author, Shankara, emphasises that happiness and suffering are mere conditions that must be transcended for attaining purification of the mind—*citasuddhi*. Herein, 'Vedanta *vicara* is synonymous with *atma-vicara*.' Having established the methodology of inquiry, Adi Shankara advances to the next level of initiation (of the seeker) with the *atman-anatman vicara*; 'knowledge and ignorance must have the same object and same locus'. In this way, with *Aparokshanubhuti*, the Acharya prods the seeker to take the first step of Advaita Vedanta.

Directed only by the tradition of reason and experience instead of 'philosophical speculation', the seeker is led by Advaitin Shankara in the search for the Self. Exhibiting his pedagogy, verse 16 reads: 'As I am also the One, the Subtle, the Knower, the Witness, the Ever-Existent, and the Unchanging, so there is no doubt that I am "that" (i.e., *Brahman*). Such is this enquiry.'

Employing the five 'pointers' of differentiation, Shankara provides mundane examples in verses 17 to 39 that discuss: the *drishta-drisya* (seer-seen); the *Cit-jaddha* (sentient-insentient); the *savikaar-nirvikar* (changing-unchanging); the *saguna-nirguna* (attribute-without attribute), and the *ekam-anekam* (singularity-plurality). Thus highlighting the *Veda-vakiya*, 'By the servant (mind) of the servants (sense organs), I have been made a servant.'

In order to gauge the candidate's understanding of self-inquiry, Adi Shankara elaborates upon a three-pronged evaluation, by asking the following: do I hear it, do I get it, and is it a fact. By the analysis of *atman-anatman vicara* that is heightened through scriptural testimonials, the Acharya establishes that *jiva* and *Atman* are two separate entities. The epistemology of knowledge is elegantly illustrated through the aforementioned 'pointers' of differentiation.

The terse vocabulary displayed through words like *avadhya*, *nirvadhya*, *nirabhasa*, *samtam*, *muddha*, *dehantitam*, and so on, makes *Aparokshanubhuti* a tremendously insightful text.

Almost halfway through *Aparaokshanubhuti*, just when the candidate settles about the duality of individual-*jiva*, and pure consciousness—*Atman*, Adi Shankara jolts the candidate by dissolving the distinction altogether with the stroke of non-duality. With verse 41, Acharya awakens the seeker by asking: 'Thus the enunciation of the difference between *Atman* and the body has (indirectly) asserted, indeed, after the manner of the "*Tarakshastra*", the reality of the phenomenal world. But what ends of human life are served thereby?' This is the turning point in the discourse wherein the invisible second step of Advaita Vedanta emerges.

Adi Shankara's intention with the hidden two-step approach is for the seeker to unequivocally comprehend Advaita. Realising that the aspirant's limited vision (due to ignorance) only sees through tangible distinctions ('this is my body', 'I am this', 'my life…my work', and so on), the Acharya employs dialectics for enlightening on the One-with-no-second. Shankara's use of the term '*tarakshastra*' in the text is meant for the logicians, especially the *samkhya-s*, who infer while professing about Being—*purusha*, and Nature—*prakriti*.

Henceforth in the *Aparokshanubhuti*, Adi Shankara introduces scriptural testimonials (Upanishadic statements) for upholding Advaita Vedanta as the only Truth. Verses 42 to 89 unleashes 'a battery of examples' to reinforce the wisdom of the *Upanishads*; *Brhadaryanka's* 'All this is *Atman*', *Chandogya's* 'Whatever is born of *Brahman*, remains *Brahman*', *Katho's* 'Brahmajajnam, one that is born of Brahma', *Isa's* 'As the indwelling, Self (of all), I am all this'.

Unsparingly, the Advaitin Adi Shankara instructs on the falsity and futility of *avidya* that can only be dispelled by *jnana* that eventually leads to *moksha*; Advaita Vedanta delivers liberation while living—*jivan mukti*.

Aparokshanubhuti's verses 89 to 99 illuminate *jivan mukti* by bringing into the discourse the theory of works (*karma*). The text says: 'If the ignorant still arbitrarily maintains this, they will not only involve themselves in two absurdities but will also run the risk of foregoing the Vedantic conclusion. So one should accept those *shrutis* alone from which proceeds true knowledge'. Echoing the instruction of *Atma Advaitam*, through this verse, Shankara draws the candidate's attention towards *prarabhdha karma* in Advaita Vedanta.

The subsequent verse 100 is of paramount significance as the enlightened Advaitin Shankara offers fifteen practices for the candidate to contemplate upon Advaita through practice: *sravana*, *mananna*, and *nidhiadhyasa*. Encapsulated herein is the gist of Adi Shankara's integrated Advaita Vedanta. It is inclusive of techniques from the *Patanjali Yoga Sutra* and offers 15 steps for Self-realisation:

i. *Yama*—control of the senses;

ii. *Niyama*—control of mind;

iii. *Tyaga*—renunciation;

iv. *Mauna*—Quietude;

v. *Desha*—place or space;

vi. *Kaal*—time;

vii. *Asana*—posture;

viii. *Moolbandha*—the root that restrains;

ix. *Dehasamya*—equipoise of the body;

x. *Driksthiti*—steadiness of vision;

xi. *Pranasyamana*—control of vital forces;

xii. *Pratyahar*—self withdrawal;

xiii. *Dharana*—concentration;

xiv. *Atmadhyana*—meditation on *Atman*;

xv. *Samadhi*—complete absorption.

This concise instruction, according to Adi Shankara, is the key to Vedantic well-being. *Aparoskanubhuti's* verses 102 to 134 explain each of the above-mentioned 15 ways to know one's real self. In the concluding section of the text, the Acharya employs the analogy of pot-clay to reinforce the 'source code' of Advaita Vedanta. Verses 135 to 139 speak of the basic methodology of Advaita, explained through the phenomena of cause and effect. It accentuates that 'IS'-ness of Reality (*Brahman*) transcends space, time, and object dimension.

The text, *Aparokshanubhuti*, through phenomenological experience, reveals its identity as *jnana prakaranagrantha* in verses 140 to 144, wherein the 15-step manual of *raja yoga* and *hatha yoga* coalesce into *jnanayoga.* Thereby giving options to both kinds of spiritual candidates—defaulters and the enlightened.

Although each of Adi Shankara's handbooks deals with the tenets of Advaita, the distinguishing feature of these writings is the style in which they have been presented. From the sternness of a disciplined Acharya in some to an endearing *guru* in others, the poetical *prakarana-grantha*, as a genre, enjoys mass appeal that responds to 'music, dance, and hymn-singing in ecstasy'. For such an audience, the Great Master's inquiry on *Brahman*—'That Pure existence', formless and without parts, Infinite and '*nivisesa*', *svyam-cit*, can be grasped through non-dual works like *Aparokshanubhuti.* The following verse from the said text highlights the foundational facts (two-step approach) of Advaita as formulated by Adi Shankara.

> One should verily see the cause in the effect,
> and then dismiss the effect altogether.
> What then remains, the sage himself becomes. (139)

In his decoding of Advaita through *nama-rupa* illustration, that neither are the particular objects 'real' nor 'unreal'; but are '*anirvacaniya*'—indescribable, the Advaitin Shankara is mentoring directly on monism. Furthermore, he is of the view that *avidya* or *ajnana* can be explained through (i) the concealment of the truth—*Avarana* and (ii) the distortion of the truth—*Viksepa.* However, '*The Brahman,* the hidden Self in everyone, doesn't shine forth. It is revealed to those who keep their mind one-pointed on the Lord of love, and thus develop—super-conscious manner of knowing.' (Sri Sri Ravi Shankar)

Stotra-s

Sahitya's last segment highlights Adi Shankara's famous poetry, reflected in his *stotra* writings. As the innovative Acharya and an endearing Advaitin, Shankara's *stotra* writings are reflective of his devotion towards the female form of the Divine, popularly manifested as devi/shakti. Having lost his father at a very young age, Shankara was deeply attached to his mother, Aryamba. It is believed that his lyrical compositions, the *stotra-s*, have roots in his relationship with his mother. Employed to a variety of musical metres, it is estimated that the poet Shankara composed 1500 to 1800 *stotra-s* mostly during the course of his *Yatra*—travels. Hence, these form a vital genre of his writings as well as prove to be a distinct domain of study of Advaita Vedanta. Covering an extensive range of themes and subjects, each *stotra* encapsulates Adi Shankara's central teaching rendered musically.

Whether it is the distinguished contribution of his Advaita *vicara* or the arduous undertaking of his *digvijaya-yatra*, Adi Shankara's *stotra-s* accomplished a great deal. In the repertoire of Acharya's writings, as a genre, these poetic renditions became extraordinary literary gems, sung and enjoyed by commoners who thronged temples and other sites.

'Knowledge can never be the object of a command. If it is, it can be but an action, like contemplation'—a statement Adi Shankara made during his scriptural debate—*shastrartha* with Mandana Misra; as chronicled by another prominent Vedantin, Madhavacharya, also a well-known biographer of the Acharya. In light of this statement, a brief examination of Shankara's *stotra-s* is recommended, given the relevance and popularity of these 'pious accoutrements'; both in philosophical literature and devotional music, to date.

An interesting observation made by scholar Lakshmi Chithambaran during the online symposium, *Global Festival of Oneness* 2020, posited the importance of Shankara's *stotra sahitya,* by saying, 'Acharya gives complete freedom to the seeker(s); read whatever you want in order to begin your inward journey; as if saying "in whatever you read I will make sure that you find *Tat Tvam Asi*".'

Another scholar, K. Ramasubramanian, observed, 'The brilliance of his unmatched skill as a poet and a philosopher is merged, quite like Advaita in the *sabd* and *artha alankar*; the key elements of his *stotra-s*. Some of the hymns are elaborate, while others are pithy and succinct. From a philosopher's standpoint, Adi Shankaracharya provides the orthodox—*karam kandins* a vast landscape of *bhakti* within the fold of non-duality.' The *sabdalanakar* in *Sri Ganesapancaratnam* accentuates the poet Shankara's unique vocabulary, combined with blazing clarity of thought. The selected *stotra-s* for the book in hand display Shankara's deep adoration for the deified Ganesha, Shiva, Vishnu, and Goddess Amba. While studying these writings, it was interesting to observe that the stern commentator and disciplinarian, Acharya Adi Shanakara, effortlessly settles in as the devotionally impassioned poet; thereby highlighting *bhakti* as a path to Self-realisation.

According to some intellectuals, the nature of the *stotra-s* is 'benevolent' because of the sentiment of devotional diversity the hymns represent. With respect for the Indian pantheon of gods and goddesses, Acharya Shankara's expansive collection of hymns offers 'each one for each kind'. Apart from the technical aspects of structure and style that lend appeal, it is the motifs chosen by the poet Shankara that heighten their importance centuries later. The four *matthas* founded by Adi Shankara are instances of the living Vedantic traditions wherein these hymns are central to the daily functioning of the spiritual centres.

Highlighting the aspect of devotion in Advaita, as per his integrated idea of non-duality (*jnana, karma, bhakti* lead to *moksha*), the Acharya's verses glorify personal gods, the deified statues of temples and shrines. For instance, the concluding *stotra* of *Subrahmaniyabhujangam* reflects the poet's *dasya bhakti*, seeking forgiveness from the divine with the analogy of parents forgiving their child for having committed *aparadha* (inappropriate deed). The same *stotra* also displays Adi Shankara's literary talent as a devotee pleading at Thrissur's sea-facing temple. The poetic *alankar* in the description of undulating tides, allegorically posited for the *bhakt* who braves '*apada*' dangers to reach the deity, juxtaposed with the snails on the shore as teachers instructing mortals to remain steadfast on the path of *bhakti*, exudes the Advaitin's seminal intellect.

Among the most popular of compilations is the hundred-verse compilation *Shivanandalahari*, considered by many as 'the greatest poetic prayer couched in an undercurrent of practical philosophy'. Poet Shankara, through the anthology, exhausts all measures of devoutness and *sringara rasa* in praise of the Adi Yogi Shiva of the Cosmic *Sivam.* The *stotra-s* in the said collection express varying moods and emotions of the devotee, from the agonising pain of separation to scathing sarcasm at the pretentious lot immersed in ritualistic fervour (hymn 9) to occasions of humour seeking the indulgence of the One-with-no-second (hymn 32).

gabhire kasare visati vijane ghor- vipine
vishale shaile cha brahmathi kusumartha jada mathi I
samarpy'aikam ceta-sarasijam umanatha bhavate
sukhena 'vasthatum jana iha na janati kim aho II 9 II

Searches and hunts the dim-witted one,
In the deep dark lake, In the lonely
dangerous forest, And in the broad high
mountains For a flower to worship thee.
It is a wonder, That these people do not
know, To offer to you the single lotus,
From the lake of one's own mind,
Oh God who is the consort of Uma,
And be happy at one's own place.

jvalograh sakala'mara'ti bhayada ksvelah kadam va tvaya
drustah kim ca kare dhruta karatale kim pakva jambu-phalam I
jihvayam nihitas'-ca siddha-ghutika va kanta-dese bhrtah
kim te nilamani vibusanam ayam sambho mahatman vada II 32 II

How was the fierce flame like poison
Which made all the courageous devas fear,
Seen by you, my Lord?
Was that fire carried in your hand,
Did it appear like the fully ripe plum fruit to you?
Was it not kept on your tongue,
Did it appear as pills from the Siddha doctor?
Was it not worn in your neck,
Did it appear like a blue gem ornament to you?
Oh, Shambhu the great one, be pleased to tell.

Composed in the *Aryavarta* metre, stanza 69 is unique because of the unmitigated poetic audacity exhibited in the wistful yet poignant description of the deified Shiva. The utterly unapologetic manner in which the verse begins detailing the strange ornamentation of deified Shiva resonates with the unconventional Advaitin Shankara: Adi Yogi's ash-smeared body covered with an inanimate tiger-deer skin, adorning a blemished crescent in his locks and the crooked gaited serpent in the neck. At the same time, the hymn closes with the Poet's humble submission as an ardent devotee.

jadata pasuta kalankita
kutila-caratwam ca naasti mayi deva I
asti yadi Rajamoule,
bhavad-abharanasya na-'smi kim patram II 69 II

The bold display of diverse emotions enveloped with precision evokes heartfelt appreciation for the exceptional poet. Contrastingly, stanza 28 of the collection speaks of the non-dual cosmic reality addressed as *Shivam*, wherein the Advaitin and Acharya in the Poet Shankara arise with vigour. The ingenuity evident in *stotra sahitya* is at par with the dexterity of his commentaries; a rare accomplishment by all standards.

sarupyam tava pujana siva mahadeveti sankirtane
samipyam siva-bhakti-dhurya-janatha-sangatya-sambhasane I
salokyam cha caracarathmaka tanudyane bhavanipate
sayujyam mama siddham atra bhavati svamin
krtartho'smyaham II 28 II

O lord of Bhavani! I attain to similarity of form with Thee by performing thy ritualistic worship; to closeness with Thee by singing Thy praise; to residence in Thy heavenly plane by associating conversing with Thy noble devotees; and to oneness with Thee by contemplating on Thy form constituted of the whole of this living and non- living world. Thus in this very embodiment I shall attain life's fulfilment.

Exploration of Adi Shankara's poetic writings can be an overwhelming endeavour because, within the literal and the spiritual meaning of each *stotra*, interpretations can be drawn at various levels. To that extent, the awakened poet has persevered to engage every being as a candidate, seeking a metaphysical connection. The following *stotra-s* reflect the *bhakt* Adi Shankara's sincerity and a poet's concern for humanity.

vaturva gehi va yatir api jati va taditaro
naro va ya kascid bhavatu bhava kim tena bhavati I
yadiyam hrt- padmam yadi bhavad-adhinam pasupate
tadiya stvam sambho bhavasi bhava-bharam ca vahasi II 11 II

Be it a celibate seeker of truth,
Be it a man of the family, Be it
a shaven-headed seeker of truth,
Be it the matted-haired householder
in the forest, Or be it one who is none
of these, Hey, Lord of all beings, If his
lotus heart is in your custody, Shambho,
You would wholly become his, And help
him to lift, This heavy burden of life.

guhayam gehe va bahi api vane va'adri-sikhare
jale va vahnau va vasatu vasateh kim vada phalam I
sada yasy'aiva'ntah karanam api sambho tava pade
sthitam ced yogo'sau sa ca parama-yogi sa cha sukhi II 12 II

Be it in a cave, Be it in house,
Be it outside, Be it in a forest,
Be it in the top of a mountain,
Be it in water, Be it in fire,
Please tell, What does it matter,
Where he lives?
Always, if his inner mind,
Rests on the feet of Shambhu,
It is Yoga and He is the greatest Yogi
And he will be happy forever...

Based on *jnana yoga*, the Advaita Vedanta provides the freedom to a *bhakt* to be a *darshanik* and vice versa, that is, a philosopher to be a devotee. Indicative of the *atma-anatma vicara* or the undisclosed first step of the Advaita, stanza 61 in *Shivanandalahari* amplifies the nuance as follows:

ankolam nija-bija santhatir ayaskantopalam sucika
sadhvi naija-vibhum lata kshitiruham sindhuhsaridvallabham I
prapnotiha yatha tatha pasupateh padaravinda dvaiyam
cetovrtti roopetya tishtati sada sa bhakthir ity ucyate II

Like the real seed progeny reaches for the mother ankola tree,
Like the iron needle reaches for the lodestone.
Like the chaste woman reaches for her lord,
Like the tender creeper reaches for nearby trees,
Like the river reaches for the sea,
If the spirit of the mind,
Reaches for the lotus feet of Pasupati,
And stays there always,
Then that state is called devotion.

Adi Shankara, through his *stotra-s,* emphasises that an aspirant's worship of the formless, attributeless Supreme Being is sublimated to a God with forms, attributes, and characteristics, which remains non-dual in principle. While discoursing on devotion, the ancients proclaimed that '*Japa* is the best *Dharma* of all *Dharmas*'; another significant aspect that the Great Master's *stotra sahitya* accomplishes. The following hymn 77 of the *Shivanandalahari* echoes the same idea:

buddhi sthira bhavithum iswara-padapadma-
saktha vadhur virahini 'va sada smaranti I
sad-bhavana-smarana-darsana-kirtanadi
sammohit'eva siva mantra-japena vinte II

My mind to get fixed on the lotus feet of the Lord,
Resembles the sweetheart separated from her lover,
And always remembers, has sweet dreams,
Recollects of early meetings and sings about it,
And in similar fashion chants the names of Lord Shiva,
In a trance and gets worried.

The *Shivanandalahri* concludes with the reinforcement of the core instruction of Vedanta, the One-without-second; the Supreme Being—*Brahman.*

stothrenala maham pravachmi na mrusha deva virinchadaya,
sthutyanam gananaprasanga samaye twam agra ganyam vidhoo I
mahatmyagra vichaarana prakarane dhanathushasthomavath,
dhoothaas twam vidhuruthhamotham phalam shambho bavat
sevaka II 100 II

Oh Shambhu, all this praise I feel is enough, Though I
never wrote anything that is false. When Lord Brahma
and other Gods, List all the great Gods, They always put you
as first. And when your devotees search for the greatest God,
The other gods are moved away like the chaff from the grain,
And you are reckoned as the best among best of all grains.

Another popular hymn is the *Dakshinamurthi stotram* that signifies an ideal relationship between a teacher and his disciple. Attributed to Adi Shankara, verse 3, in particular, reveals the import of *brahmajnana* as delivered by the Acharya himself.

citram vatta-taror-muule vrddhaah shissyaa gurur-yuvaa I
guros-tu maunam vyaakhyaanam shissyaas-tuc-chinna-samshayaah II

It is indeed a strange picture to behold; At the root (i.e. base) of
a Banyan Tree (Vata) are seated old Disciples (i.e. aged Disciples)
in front of a Young Guru, The Guru is Silent, and Silence is His
exposition (of the Highest Knowledge); and that (Silence is severing
the doubts (automatically) from the minds of the Disciples.

The concise expression of the scriptures is evident in all of the ten *stotra-s* of *Dakshinamurti*, a recommended text for the musically inclined candidate who is prepared to abide by non-duality through unconditional devotion.

visam darpandrsyamananagaritulyam nijatargatam
pasyannatmani mayaya bahirivodbhutam yatha nidraya I
yah saksatkurute prabodhasamaye svatmanmevadvayam

tasmai srigurumurtaye nama idam sridaksinamurtaye II

I bow to Shri Dakshinamurti in the form of my guru:
I bow to him. By whose grace the whole of the world is found to
exist entirely in the mind, Like a city's image mirrored in a glass.
Though like a dream, through Maya's power it appears outside;
and by whose grace, again, on the dawn of, Knowledge, it is
perceived as the everlasting and non-dual self.

The power to choose or 'free will' is a discretionary attribute that needs utmost discipline whilst being executed. It is indeed amusing that, fulfilling his *pravrtti-dharma* and immersed in materialism, the individual exploits the attribute to the fullest. However, in the most crucial endeavour of realising his real nature, blatant inertia consumes his intellect—*buddhi*, and he continues to revel in ignorance. Anticipating the individual's waking from sleep (of ignorance), Adi Shankara, through his poetic writings, provides ample ways and means to 'do something about it'.

In *Vivekacunamai*, Adi Shankara proclaims that *bhakti* is the greatest support to Advaita Vedanta. He is recognised for the contribution of six systems of worship, hence, is also called '*shanmata sthapanacharya*'; 'For worship assumes as its object some form' (Woodroffe). In *Saundarya Lahari* ('The Wave of Beauty'), widely recognised as 'one of the greatest classical pieces of devotional poetry', are stanzas glorifying Shaktism. The collection has over a hundred *stotra-s*, categorised under *Ananda Lahari* (first 41 stanzas) and *Saundarya Lahari* (next 52 stanzas), eulogising the Goddess Lalithambika, incarnate of Goddess Parvati, the consort of Shiva. The following metrical *stotra-s* 45 and 56 illustrate the Poet's beatific and symbolic expression:

aralaih swabhavyadalikalabha-sasribhiralakaih
paritham the vakhtram parihasati pankheruha-ruchim I
dara-smere yasmin dasana-ruchi-kinjalka-ruchire
sugandhau madhyanti Smara-dahana-chaksur-madhu-lihah II

By nature slightly curled,
And shining like the young honey bees
Your golden thread-like hairs,

Surround your golden face.
Your face makes fun of the beauty of the lotus.
And adorned with slightly parted smile,
Showing the tiers of your teeth,
Which are like the white tendrils,
And which are sweetly scented.
Bewitches the eyes of God,
Who burnt the god of love.

tav'aparne karne-japa-nayana-paisunya-chakita
niliyante thoye niyatham animeshah sapharikah I
iyam cha srir baddhasc-chada-puta-kavaiam kuvalayam
jahati pratyupe nisi cha vighatayya pravisathi II

Oh, She who is begotten to none,
It is for sure,
That the black female fish in the stream,
Are afraid to close their eyes.
Fearing that thine long eyes,
Resembling them all,
Would murmur bad about them,
In your ears to which they are close by.
It is also for sure,
That the Goddess Lakshmi,
Enters the blooming blue Lilly flowers,
Before your eyes close at night,
And reenter in the morn when they open.

It is interesting to observe that both anthologies, namely, the *Shivananada Lahari* and *Saundarya Lahari*, share certain similarities. Both have the same number of hymns (100), both are eulogies to the divine, both enjoy symbolic references to nature, and both focus on a comparable range of themes and emotions reflective of Adi Shankara immersed in devotion.

Composed during Acharya's travels, both are illustrative of the life and mores experienced by him with sensitivity and responsibility. According to Adi Shankara, 'tradition means safeguarding knowledge encased in lifestyle', and his *stotra sahitya* is indicative of his dedication towards the ordinary folk; a constrained living yet upholding the values and customs of society that are kindness, goodness, and collective harmony. His writings reveal that he saw futility in academic discoursing of *Isvara* and was more inclined towards 'reviving and revising', in order to realise wholesome—*sampoortvum* status of self.

'Sayings give information and advice to men of the world, whilst *Mantras* awaken superhuman power or Sakti. A mere saying is therefore, like a *Jiva*, subject to birth and death, whilst a *Mantra* is directly *Brahman* in sound-body, unwasting and undecaying.' (Woodroffe) Thus, *Saundarya Lahari* is actually a remarkable specimen of Adi Shankara's writing that delves into the dimensions of *Mantra*, *Yantra*, and *Tantra* as reflected in the following *stotra-s* 26 and 27:

virincih panchatvam vrajati harir apnoti virathim
vinasam kinaso bhajati dhanado yati nighanam I
vitandri mahendri vithathir api sammeelita-drsa
maha-samhare smin viharati sati tvat-patirasau II

The creator reaches the dissolution,
The Vishnu attains death,
The god of death even dies,
Kubera the lord of wealth expires,
The Indras close their eyes one after one,
And attain the wakeless sleep,
During the final deluge,
But you my chaste mother,
Play with your consort the Sadashiva.
27

japo jalpah shilpam sakalam api mudra-virachana
gatih pradaksinya-kramanam asanady'ahuti-vidhih I
pranamah samvesah sukham akilam atmarpana-drsa
saparya-paryayas tava bhavatu yan me vilasitam II

Let the mutterings that I do,
With the sacrifice in my soul.
Become chanting of your name,

Let all my movements become thine Mudhras,
Let my travel become perambulations around thee,
Let the act of eating and drinking become fire sacrifice to thee,
Let my act of sleeping becomes salutations to you,
And let all actions of pleasure of mine,
Become parts of thine worship.

The assortment of concerns addressed in the *Saundarya Lahari* is astonishing. From the description of the goddess to adulation to seeking affection, knowledge, strength, peace, health, prosperity, and so on, the text is insightful. Each *stotra* reverberates with *bhakti-bhava* and is sculpted with literary fluency in comprehensible Sanskrit. In *stotra* 51, the poetic element of *'ullekha'* is accentuated, wherein the poet and devotee Shankara's *stuti* pivots on a multitude of interpretations drawn from a mere glance.

shive sringarardhra tad-ithara-jane kutsana-paraa
sarosha Gangayam Girisa-charite'vismayavathi I
har'ahibhyo bhita sarasi-ruha-saubhagya-janani
sakhishu smera the mayi janani dristih sakaruna II

(Quiescent) Mother! Thy look is amorous with love towards Siva, Contemptuous towards others, full of anger against Ganga, Astonished and quiescent of Siva's lilas (deportment), Frightened on seeing the snakes of Hara, Triumphant over the grace of the lotus and smiling at Her comrades. Towards me it is full of grace.

The *Saundarya Lahari* can prove to be a technical text for the non-initiated because several stanzas of the text concern *Sri Vidya* and the influence of *Sri Chakra* in Advaita Vedanta. *Stotra* 11 of *Saundarya Lahari* highlights the import:

chaturbhih shri-kantaih shiva-yuvatibhih panchabhir api
prabhinnabhih sambhor navabhir api mula-prakrthibhih I
chatus-chatvarimsad vasu-dala-kalasra-trivalaya-
tri-rekhabhih sardham tava sarana-konah parinatah II

> Thy abode of nine angles—four of Siva and five of Sakti—together
> With eight petals, sixteen leaves, three roundings, and three walls,
> enlarges itself into one of the forty-four angles!

Music exercises tremendous influence on the organ of the mind predominantly, and other sensory organs as well, because of the *urja* (energy) it creates. Such a simplistic perspective has roots in a more profound Vedantic concept, that of *Mantra-shakti*. 'When the Sakti with attribute, resident in and as the *Mantra*, is by dint of *Sadhana* awakened, then She opens the gate of monistic truth, revealing the true nature and essence of the universe' (Woodroffe). Poet Shankara's *Saundarya Lahari* bears this very quintessence.

'Mental bath is meditation upon Vishnu,' says *Vishnu Sahasranama*, containing 142 verses, extracted from Shanti Parva in the 149th chapter of the *Mahabharata*, in the dialogue between Bhishma and Yudhishtira. Acharya wrote a commentary on *Vishnu Sahasranama* that focuses on *bhakti* through contemplation in the absence of any religious ceremony, is unlike any other theological form of devotion, is beyond time or space constraint, and does not seek preparation or qualification of any kind from the devotee.

In the introductory chapter of Acharya's commentary on the *Vishnu Sahasranama*, Yudhishtira asks Bhishma, 'What is that *Dharma* which is regarded by you as the supreme one among all *Dharmas*? By reciting what (Hymn) is mankind freed from the bonds of birth and *samsara*?' Quoting the *Manusmriti* (2-85), Acharya Shankara writes, '*Reciting*: *Japa* is of threefold nature, *viz.*, loud, audible, and mental'. Further, with the introductory verse 6, the Poet Shankara illustrates the seeking of liberation through *japa* by saying:

> *anadi-nidhanam Visnum sarva-loka-mahesvaram I*
> *lok'adhyaksham stuvan nityam sarva-dukhatigo bhavet II*

> By always praising Vishnu, who is without beginning or
> end who is the Supreme Lord of all the worlds, and who
> is the observer of the Universe one gets beyond all grief

Adi Shankara's *Vishnu Sahasranamastotram* is a lyrical construct based on the scriptural truth of the *Bhagavadgita* that states: '*Anything that is glorious, brilliant, or powerful is a manifestation of my effulgence.*' The opening verse of the *Vishnu Sahasranama Stotram* begins with the first of the thousand names of Vishnu, *Visvam*, meaning the Universe; it also captures commentator Shankara's Advaita:

om visvam visnur vasat-karo bhuta-bhavya-bhavat-prabhuh I
bhutakrd bhutabhrd bhavo bhutatma bhuta-bhavanah II

A part of the summary of Acharya's *bhasya* verse 1 reads as follows, '*Visvam*: The All. He whom the *Upanishads* indicate by the passage '*Yatah sarvani bhutani*' as the cause of the generation, sustentation, and dissolution of the universe. Or alternatively, as the universe has no existence apart from him, He can be called *Visvam,* The Universe. In support of it are the Upanishadic statements: *Brahma ev'edam visvam idam varishtam*—this universe is verily the supreme *Brahman* (Mu. Up. 2-2-11). *Purusa ev'edam visvam*—this universe is the Purusa Himself (Mu. Up. 2-1-10).'

The *stotram* details every aspect of the Cosmic Vishnu, especially in the use of the word *amaya,* suggestive of the Divine as *saguna* and *nirguna.* The mention of a thousand names of the formless Vishnu is the import of Advaita, asking the devout to meditate with the purity of his entire being.

Non-duality and Duality are not at the same level. However, Advaita, as propagated by Adi Shankara, is about the duality that exists within the non-dual *vicara.* Therefore, for an inquirer who is far removed from the Veda-Vedanta discourse, devotion is a much-valued opening for Self-realisation. For the simple-minded commoner, Adi Shankara's poetry links the ignorant, the lost, to the One—Absolute Reality waiting in silence inside a temple's sanctum.

Practical Vedanta: All or Nothing

Deeds and decisions wrap or trap us endlessly. It is rare that an opportunity to cease and see occurs. The occasion to script on Adi Shankara and Advaita remains one such rarity. Undeniably, the writing of which, on all accounts, has proved to be a paradigm shift for me. Engagement with its subject made certain fundamentals distinctly clear, more so at a point in time when such clarity rescued me from getting lost. To the inquirer/reader, I can only hope that sharing these encourages a moment of quietude and sight for you as well.

- Change the narrative.
- Do not dwell on the past; use it for the experience it provides.
- Habits tend to turn into fixations. Be aware.
- Refrain from postponements.
- Respond with care. Begin with yourself.
- The Present alone matters. Use it fully.
- Hesitation hinders.
- Instead of asking why me, rephrase by saying why not me.

Living with the aid of these instructions has allowed me to tide over episodes of major trials that include losing both parents in quick succession. Blessed with a beautiful life, it is difficult not to fulfil the urge to return bountifully. Without getting intimidated by the measure of intention, a reworking of myself all the time allows me to look at the inadequacies vividly. Realising that 'Nothing comes alone', hence the 'pair of opposites'—good and bad, joy and sorrow, and so on, relieves me of unwanted egotistical hang-ups.

Co-habitating with solitude has been a powerful learning experience. My abode is my classroom. It bestows All that I need and removes absolutely Nothing that is remotely inconsequential.

Conclusion

'Life is like a landscape. You live in the midst of it, but can describe it only from the vantage point of distance.'

—Charles Linderbergh

Philosophy in Hindi is called *darsana*, and in Sanskrit, *vidya*. Both the words qualify for an aspirational seeking with profundity as a key element of understanding. An elevated sphere of activity, Philosophy necessitates the presence of order, ethics, and direction. It is therefore a natural denominator for all pursuits.

In the present age of technological dominance, both philosophy and wellness/well-being are underutilised. Given that the thought evolves with the course of thinkers' own life stories, an attempt has been made through this book to coalesce the two dynamics, namely, Adi Shankara and his thought of Advaita. Hailed as 'first of his rank', in my view, he remains a remarkable thinker whose life *is* his work; dictated by the principle of 'personal sacrifice for the sake of the majority'.

Adi Shankara, Advaita, and You is an attempt to showcase the sagacious spiritual principle through dimensions that are integral to his personality: his *vicara*, *digvijaya*, and *sahitya*. For restoring spiritual order in a chaotic and hostile environment, he decoded a highly advanced science (of Advaita), persevered for its spread by walking the vastly divergent landscape, and built bridges of communication through Dialogue. Both activities (walking and dialogue), in my understanding, are exemplary of human perseverance and deliverance. Perhaps, now more than ever before, there is a need for reconnecting and adopting both of these for the pursuit of self-inquiry.

It would not be an exaggeration to state that Adi Shankara lived fulfilling his responsibility—*dharma*—as a mortal. With the establishment of the *peetha-s*, he brought the mighty *Mahavakya-s* to the doorstep of aspirants and devotees alike. His *darshanik drishti* (philosopher's insight), evident through his writings, delivered the opportunity for *moksha* while living. For *anubhava* of the Self which lies beyond *antahkarana* and *buddhi*, the enlightened renunciate offered *srvana, mananna*, and *nityadhyasa*. In the sphere of higher learning, the popular dictum, '*Jano ya Mano*' (experience with reason or believe without inquiry), indicates the direction a beginner takes. The expanse of his writings indicates that Acharya Shankara clearly adheres to '*Jano*' as does his Advaita.

In the realm of Vedanta, Shankara's stature is intimidating for scholars of Advaita as well as the practising Vedantins. As an Acharya, his focus while imparting *jnana* was not only on the accurate interpretation of the Scriptures but also on making the import simple for his students with modest backgrounds.

In *Vakya vrtti*, a text by Shankara in the form of a dialogue between the guru and his *shishya*, he defines *bhasya* as:

sutrartho varnyate yatra padaih sutranusaribhih
svapadani ca varnyate bhasyam bhasyavido viduh I

'*Bhasya* is a literature in which Acharya not only explains every word in the *mantra* (statements of the scriptures) but also explains his own words, inasmuch as he has to logically convince the students why he has interpreted words of the *mantra* as he has done'. For the teacher, Adi Shankara, who taught non-duality with love, patience, and in the absence of prejudice, Swami Vivekananda states, 'He was one of the last of its representatives.'

The advocacy for Adi Shankara's Advaita, as addressed in the book in hand, is hugely relevant today. Amidst the global environment of hatred, hostility, and fear, his is a voice that compels questioning mindlessness and blatant ignorance. More importantly, the instrument needed is available 'right here, right now'; the non-contact *yoga* or '*asparsa yoga*' referred to by

Acharya Gaudapada in his *Mandukya Karika* as (3.39) and about which Shankara comments in his *bhasya* by saying:

> *'This Yoga, which is not in touch with anything, is hard to be attained by all Yogis (in general). The Yogis are afraid of it, for they see fear in it where there is really fearlessness.'*

Elucidating upon his *dada-guru's* (Acharya Gaudapada) Advaita teaching, Shankara writes in verse 39 of his commentary on the *Mandukya*: 'The word "*Yoga*" signifying union, generally means contact between two. But derivatively, *Jnana-Yoga* is not in touch with any idea or object, as there exists nothing else but the non-dual *Brahman*. Therefore, it is called the *Asparsa-Yoga*, i.e., a spiritual discipline which does not admit of relation or touch with anything else.' Advaita is *Asparsa-Yoga*. It is the wisdom about the Absolute Being in the absence of contact or touch perceived typically, as the object and subject (mind-body framework).

Under the unusual circumstances of a pandemic, the availability of contactless wisdom may appear surreal to some. The attitudes that emerged across geography, ethnicity, and cultural backgrounds were meant to be driven by compassion, care, and concern. It was imagined that an invisible virus could prompt a new philosophy and forge new social solidarities. However, since 2020, the world as we know it continues to experience more than one intercontinental conflict, countless deaths have occurred as a result of man-made disasters, and a savage-like, rampant urge to fulfil desires appears to have consumed most of us. What did we learn?

> *naham manusyo na ca deva yaksau*
> *na brahmana ksatriya vaisya sudrah*
> *na brahmacari na grhi vanastho*
> *bhiksurna caham nijabodha rupah*
>
> I am not a human, demigod or a demon.
> I am not a thinker, a warrior, a trader, or a labourer.
> I am not a student, a householder, a retiree or a saint.
> I am formless, the nature of consciousness.
>
> —*Hastamalaka Stotram, verse 2*

Having concluded my walk with the text of *Adi Shankara, Advaita and You*, as an inquirer, I hope that the Advaitin Acharya's primal instruction of 'the way to get started is to quit talking and begin doing', stirs the mind-body-*atman* of anyone keen to learn and live out. Spiritual stamina and mindfulness in living are not easy practices to develop and follow. However, it is not impossible, and that is the *beej jnaan* that the author has realised.

Acknowledgements

Adi Shankara, Advaita and You owes its existence to the might of time, the support of every being and presence that orbited during its working, and the blessed environment that ensured its completion. In guidance, with humility and gratitude, it is presented for reflection to anybody and everybody who decides to inquire. The writing of the book and its completion during the Pandemic is an experiential admission that *anything is possible*.

From the moment the task of scripting on Adi Shankara and his idea of Advaita was assigned to me in early February of 2017, to the morning of 1 May 2025, when I received the email confirming the acceptance of the manuscript for publication, the struggle has been to 'subdue' my own self. Even though I was convinced of the fact that this work came for my betterment, hesitation, loss, and grief have been milestones difficult to ignore through the working of the title. The 'You' rubbled towards realising to 'function in a spirit of dispassion and detachment', with the sole companionship of gratitude. It is with the same sentiment that, as the author, I feel privileged to introduce the participants whose presence in my life, trust, and encouragement made the book possible.

The indulgent tutoring I am fortunate to receive from my niece, Lavanya Aditi Puri, and nephew, Imaad Mohan Puri, in my endeavours as a writer, encourages me to stay the course; more so in the case of this book's writing and the trying period of anticipation that preceded its publication. Thank you for not giving up on me.

I extend my heartfelt gratitude to dearest friends whose patience I have managed to exhaust on most occasions, but whose affection and admiration remain unaffected and steadfast. Thank you for not abandoning me.

Amidst the numerous drafts and redrafts the manuscript underwent, for the ad nauseam pestering that my scholar friend Manisha Gangahar ungrudgingly faced, I thank you for being dearly supportive and forthcoming with your time and patience.

Among the many unimaginables and unforgetables that *Adi Shankara, Advaita and You* experienced, one deserves special mention. Her detailed and valuable feedback on the manuscript and the spontaneous offer of an endorsement for the book furthered my strength in myriad ways. Thank you, dear Arundhanthi Subramanium, for the encouragement, friendship, and, most of all, your recommendation.

To esteemed scholar and author Veena Sharma, I am indebted for her spontaneous response in lending words of encouragement for the book. Thank you for your graciousness.

For scanning historical inaccuracies and lending an honest view regarding the treatment of the subject, I extend my sincere gratitude to author Raghavan Srinivasan, whose insightful opinion helped me reshape certain segments of the work.

The specially designed images in *Adi Shankara, Advaita and You* form a distinct part of its journey. Aside from breaking the tedium of an intense read, they are meant to convey the subtlety of the theme. To the illustrator, Gayatri Garg, thank you for your uncomplaining support and artistic contribution.

An association close to my heart since childhood is the affinity with radio. The companionship that *Vividh Bharati* rendered during the writing of the book proved to be quite remarkable. On countless occasions, the airwaves delivered almost prophetic assistance with the choice of subjects for its daily programmes. There were instances when a word or an expression used by the presenter would release me from a frustrating mental lockdown! Soundbytes from celebrated interviews contributed in a powerful manner towards the tapestry of thoughts. Most importantly, the constant sound presence of the medium reaffirmed to me that intuitive capabilities cannot be ignored. To date, the role it plays elevates my understanding of the ordinary and respect for the mundane.

For the prompt assistance and personalised attention that enabled site visits and procurement of study material, I am extremely grateful to Randeep ji, the management, and staff at the Carnoustie Resorts. Without their unsparing support, the book would not have been possible.

For the important facilitation received from Ms Sunaina at the AC Joshi Library at Panjab University, Chandigarh, I express my deep appreciation for the trouble undertaken.

To the select families who allowed *seva* sessions for their loved ones, existing in a state of suffering, words seem inadequate to express my innermost feelings. I bow in gratitude and humility for the experiences of *Sat Cit Anand*. Salutations to Providence for granting me my wish!

The blessed environs mentioned at the beginning, which contributed significantly to the completion of this book, fall within a sizeable radius; one that includes my residence (*Hari Niwas*) and the city of my birth, Chandigarh. Designed by the Swiss-French master planner Le Corbusier as a 'biological phenomenon', Chandigarh was conceptualised as a metaphor of the human body. Furthermore, its avenues of greenery are intended to 'enable the human spirit to draw strength from its active collaboration with the forces and beauties of nature'. A non-dualistic approach that I find fascinating vis-à-vis my understanding and efforts involved towards *Adi Shankara, Advaita and You*.

For the keenness of interest that Shri Pankaj P Singh, Publisher, The Browser, so promptly expressed not only gladdens me immensely, but it reiterates my trust in the gravitas of the unexplained. Magic does happen! Thank you for taking the risk with me and the text.

A special word of heartfelt appreciation for Mehakdeep Kaur, CEO of 99beagles, for her time, pleasant disposition, and open-mindedness that have given the book its form. I would also like to extend my sincere gratitude to the talented and enthusiastic designers at The Browser, Ritika and Mudra, for their unsparing diligence.

In the end and most importantly, I prostrate in complete surrender and gratitude to the Divine, Masters, and interventions that gave me the strength, enthusiasm, and direction to write the book; as does this daughter to her Ammi-Bapu for indulging her, always, to continue walking with freedom and joy.

Bibliography

Anantakrsna, R. & Garu, K.R., Tr., *Saundarya-Lahari of Sri Sankaracharya*, 1957

Ansari, Ali, *Sufism and Beyond: Sufi Thought in the Light of Late 20th Century Science,* 1999

Byrom, Thoman, *The Heart of Awareness: A Translation of the Ashtavakra Gita,* 2001

Chalmers. David. J., essay: 'Facing Up to the Problem of Consciousness', *Journal of Consciousness Studies,* 2(3): 200–19, 1995

Chandramouli, Anuja, *Kamadeva*, 2014

Chandrika, *Kulasekhara Alwar's Sri Mukundamala: A Garland of Devotional Offerings*, 2021

Chidambaram, Kamala, Tr., *Shivanadalahri* ,1989

Chinmayananda, *Sankara: The Missionary*, 1978

Cohen, S.S., *Advaitic Sadhana or The Yoga of Direct Liberation*, 1975

Das, Gurcharan, *The Difficulty of Being Good: On the Subtle Art of Dharma*, 2009

Easwaran, Eknath, *Vishnu and His 1000 Names,* 2017

Garcia, H., & Miralles, F., *Ikigai: The Japanese Secret to a Long and Happy Life*, 2017

Geo, *The Power of Faith: Spirituality, Religion, Pilgrimage,* December 2008

Gordon, Stewart, *When Asia Was the World,* 2009

Johnson, W.J., *Oxford Dictionary of Hinduism*, 2009

Joshi, Arun, *The Last Labyrinth*, 1981

Maharshi, Ramana, *Ramana, Shankara and the Forty Verses: The Essential Teachings of Advaita*, 2002

Mayeda, Sengaku, *Sankara's Upadesasahasri: Critically Edited with Introduction and Indices,* 1973

Mudgal, S.G., *Advaita of Sankara: A Reappraisal of Buddhism and Samkhya on Sankara's Thought*, 1975

Murty, K.S., *Revelation and Reason in Advaita Vedanta*, 1959

M., Sri, *Shuniya*, 2018

Nair, P.K. Sasidharan, *Revealing Advaita Vedanta,* 2004

Nandakumar, Prema, *Adi Sankara: Finite to the Infinite*, 2013

National Geographic Magazine, *The Healing Power of Faith*, Volume 4, Issue 5, December 2016

Padhi, Laxmikanta, *Advaita Vedanta and Environmental Ethics: Some Critical Observations*, 2019–20

Panoli, V., *Adi Sankara's Vision of Reality: A Discovery of Truths Hitherto Unknown*, 2009

Parthasarathy, A., *Choice Upanishads*, 2001

Pattanaik, Devdutt & Johnson, J., *I Am Divine So Are You*, 2017

Purushottamananda, Swami Tr., *Hastamalaka Stotram of Adi Shankaracharya*, 2008

Radhakrishnan, S., *Indian Philosophy,* Volume 2 (Thane: Repro Knowledge, 2008)

Rajagopalachari, C., *Bhaja Govindam*, 1965

Raju, P.T., *Idealistic Thought of India*, 1953

Ramachandra, A., *Advaita Philosophy of Sri Adhi Sankara*, 2007

Ranganathananda, *Shankaracharya and an Untouchable: An Exposition of Manisha Panchakam*, 2009

Rao, P. Nagaraja, *Introduction to Vedanta*, 1958

Rao, Ramachandra S.K., *The Tantra of Sri-Chakra (Bhavanopinashad)*, 1983

Rao, Srinivasa, *Advaita: A Contemporary Critique*, 2012

Reddy, V. Narayan Karan, *Adi Sankara and Aurobindo*, 1992

Saikia, Arupjyoti's essay in *Seminar,* 723, November 2019

Sartre, J.P., essay: 'The Transcendence of the Ego', 1936

Sastri, A. Mahadeva, *The Bhagavad-Gita with The Commentary of Sri Sankaracharya,* 1901

Sastry, R. Ananthakrishna, *Vishnu Sahasranama* with The *Bhasya* of *Sankaracharya*, 1927

Sharma, Veena, *Advaita Vedanta and Akan: Inquiry into an Indian and African Ethos*, 2015

Shri Sharada Peetham, *Sri Chakra: Mystic Worship of Goddess*, 2005

Shulman, David's essay 'The Veda as Word, Wisdom and the World', Seminar 671, July 2015

Sikka, Sonia's essay: 'Teaching Religion and Philosophy in India'; IIC 2013–14

Singh, Kirpal, *Spirituality: What It Is*, 1975

Sri Sri Ravi Shankar, *Commentary on Upanishads, Volume 1*, 2018

Swami Atmananda, Tr., *Sri Sankara's Teachings in His Own Words*, 1958

Swami Jagadananda, Tr., *Upadeshasahasri of Sri Sankaracharya*, 1949

Swami Krishnananda, Tr., *The Mandukya Upanishad*, 1996

Swami Mumukshananda, *Pancikaranam of Sankaracharya*, 1992

Swami Nikhalananda, Tr., *The Mandukopnishad with Gaudapada's Karika and Sankara's Commentary*, 1949

Swami Nikhilananda, Tr., *Bhaja Govindam of Sri Sankaracharya*, 1976

Swami Satprakashananda, *Mind: According to Vedanta*, 1994

Swami Sharvanada, Tr., *Kena Upanishad*, 1920

Swami Swahananda, Tr., *The Chandogya Upanisad*, 1956

Swami Tapasyananda, Tr., *Sankara Digvijaya: The Traditional Life of Sri Sankaracharya* by Madhava-Vidyaranya, 1978

Swami Tapasyananda, Tr., *Mandukya Upanishad with the Commentary of Sankaracharya*, 1989

Swami Vimuktananda, Tr., *Sri Sankaracharya's Aparokshanubhuti*, 1938

Swami Vivekananda, *Selections from Swami Vivekananda*, 1957

Vedanta Treatise: The Eternities, 1978

Thapar, Romila, *Cultural Pasts: Essays in Early Indian History*, 2000

Varma, Pavan K., *Adi Shankaracharya: Hinduism's Greatest Thinker*, 2018

Vasanthakumari, V., *Sri Sankara's Bhasyagranthas: A Synthesis of Science and Spirituality*, 2013

Wolfe, Tom, *Mauve Gloves & Madmen, Clutter & Vine*, 1976

Woodroffe, John, *The Garland of Letters (Varnamala): Studies in the Mantra Shastra*, 1963

Yuvaveer Initiative, *Drop: A Novel*, 2011

Tr., *Prasnottara Ratna-Malika of Sri Sankaracharya*, 1991

Tr., *Brahma Sutra Bhasya of Sankaracharya*, 1965

Tr., *Sri Visnu Sahasranama*, 1986

Extracts from Sri Aurobindo and the Mother, *Perspectives: For a New Millennium*

Sri Sankara on Varnavyavastha & Vedic Ritualism: New Perspectives, 2019

Vakya Vrtti: Exhaustive Analysis of That Thou Art, 2006

The Bhagavadgita, 1943

Online References:

- Swami Sarvapriyanada's YouTube talks
- https://www.rarebooksocietyofindia.org
- https://www.speakingtree.in
- https://www.shankaracharya.org
- Shankarabhasya.org
- https://www.advaita-vedanta.org
- Upanishads.kenjaques.org.uk

More from The Browser

UNFOLDED: India's Air Defence from WWII to Operation Sindoor
Pankaj P Singh
ISBN: 978-93-49042-30-8

The Sacred Sound Path
P. Sesh Kumar
ISBN: 978-93-49042-84-1

Ability: Landmark Judgements on Disability Jurisprudence in India
Navdeep Singh and Shruti Bedi
ISBN: 978-93-49042-38-4

General's Jottings Rearmed: National Security, Conflicts and Strategies (Including Operation Sindoor)
Lt Gen KJ Singh
ISBN: 978-93-49042-24-7

Politics Reimagined: An Exploration of Politics Without Politicians
Maj Gen Anil Sengar and Capt Sanjay Gahlot
ISBN: 978-93-49042-29-2

India-Pakistan: The Intractable Conflict and the China Factor
Maj Gen Virender Budhwar
ISBN: 978-93-92210-73-0

Emergency and Neo-Emergency
M. G. Devasahayam
ISBN: 978-81-979897-5-9

Flowers on a Kargil Cliff
Vikram Jit Singh
ISBN: 978-81-979897-9-7

Liminal Tides
Soumitra Banerji
ISBN: 978-93-92210-64-8

Dusk over the Mustard Fields
Ranjit Powar
ISBN: 978-93-88150-10-1

For More Information